INSIGHTS

**into transvestism,
transsexualism and other
gender presentations**
contributed by
Dr. Russell Reid,
Melanie McMullen,
Stacy Novak,
Ashley Carrington et al.

Publication of Insights has been enabled thanks to
the generous provision of Development Fund monies
by our sponsors:
Basildon PCT
Billericay, Brentwood & Wickford PCT
Essex County Council.

**Published by TransLiving International,
ISBN 0 9543821**

Copyright TransLiving International, 2002
All rights reserved. No part of this publication may be reproduced, stored in a retrieval system or transmitted in any way or by any means, electronic, mechanical, photocopying, recording or otherwise, without the prior written permission of the copyright holder, other than the membership application/ donation form.
TransLiving International, PO Box 3,
Basildon, Essex, SS13 3WA, United Kingdom

STACY NOVAK WRITES ABOUT TRANSLIVING INTERNATIONAL

TransLiving was formed in 1980 as TransEssex, a small group for transvestites. A few years later its founder asked me to run it, so I became the Coordinator of a transgender group – unusual for a female born and happily remaining!

We changed its name a few years ago to reflect the reality of its evolution into an organisation with members from many different parts of the world. These days it produces a magazine, runs monthly parties and provides a range of counselling and advisory services.

– – – AND INSIGHTS

These activities all cost money. We rely on voluntary contributions to augment membership income and enable us to extend our services. We would particularly like to thank the sponsors of this publication for underwriting its print and production charges.

'Insights' is a digest of our famous 'Informal Guides' supplemented by many new articles expressing a range of opinion and insight. It is written for a predominantly UK based readership, although much of the matter is of universal relevance to anyone transgendered or affected by someone transgendered

This book is designed to be dipped into rather than read cover to cover. We hope you find it does provide valuable insights into some of the most puzzling areas of human behaviour.

TransLiving contacts:
Write to: Stacy Novak at TLI, PO Box 3, Basildon, Essex SS13 3WA.

Information and Helpline: Tel 01268 583761 (9am to 8pm Monday to Friday)

e-mail: stacy@transliving.co.uk   Website: http://www.transliving.co.uk

SECTION ONE:
TRANSVESTISM

*A series of articles concerning transvestism
and its impact on the transvestite and those around him.*

TRANSVESTISM

What is transvestism?

It is the behaviour pattern characterised by dressing in the clothes (some or all) normally associated with the opposite sex.

It is a mistake to assume that because we have one word to describe the act of cross-dressing (transvestism), that all transvestites (TVs) are the same, with the same compulsion, the same causes and same effects.

Each TV is an individual with his own reasons for cross-dressing, his own interpretations of what femininity is and his own expressions of his sexuality.

With TVs you simply cannot adopt the 'seen one, seen them all' approach.

Can it be cured or treated?

It seems not. Transvestism is remarkably persistent and seemingly not amenable to any treatment. Transvestites frequently decide to give it up in disgust --- but generally will revert to it in the future, particularly at times of stress. It is quite commonplace to hear of them throwing away their womens clothes, make-up etc. and promising their partners never to cross-dress again.

Broken promises, deceit and guilt

Those promises should be viewed with some suspicion: the intention at the time may have been fairly stated, but the compulsion to cross dress is likely to become too strong for the TV to resist and thus he may well revert to cross-dressing again, but even more secretively and with greater feelings of guilt.

It should be noted that because of the secrecy frequently surrounding a TVs habit, an apparent 'cure' may well be illusory: the TV is simply managing to conceal his cross-dressing more successfully.

The majority of TVs wish to be discreet and most of them, for most of the time, preserve their transvestism as a secret.

Indeed, many are greatly fearful of their transvestism becoming known and will go to extraordinary lengths to keep it under wraps.

The fear of exposure and disgrace can be so powerful as to have lead some TVs to commit suicide. They are vulnerable when cross-dressed and are surely deserving of tolerance, even if understanding may be more difficult. What makes their behaviour the more extraordinary is that whilst going to great lengths to hide their transvestism, most will, sooner or later, be driven to run the risk of going out cross-dressed in public. They want to pass in the real world: they derive a frisson of excitement from risk taking. It does seem to be somewhat contradictory that a person wants to keep his activities secret and also go out and run the risk of exposure: but that is the peculiarly contradictory nature of transvestism.

The fact that you discovered him may be because he half wanted you to. He might have aroused your suspicions by showing undue interest in television programmes featuring cross-dressing, or engaged you in simply fat too earnest discussion about your attitude to it.

There are other contradictions too: the typical TV is not a cissy. He may just as easily be a hard-drinking, rugby playing brickie as an effete window dresser.

He can be a real man's man – may even be homophobic – yet stick him in a skirt and he'll twirl and preen like a little girl.

A CROSS-DRESSING PARTNER – THE SUDDEN DISCOVERY

How should you have reacted when you discovered your partner cross-dressed? What's the point in finding out now? You reacted --- the real question concerns where to go from there.

Your reaction may well have reflected a complex bundle of feelings: embarrassment that gave rise to laughter; anger at having been deceived; disgust, shame and fear of other people discovering the problem. You need time to reflect on your feelings. Your partner almost certainly needs reassuring that you still love him.

Some partners pick up 'warning signs' such as rather too neatly arched, plucked eyebrows, shaven arms and legs, articles of clothing disappearing or turning up in unexpected places (bras, slips, knickers etc.), shoes that seem unaccountably stretched or clothes that seem to have split at the seams.

The discreet TV may give himself away by little 'jokes' he plays – jumping into bed wearing his wife's nightie for example.

His transvestism may be limited to wearing knickers. It could extend to the whole shebang. You simply need to find out all you can.

Perhaps the most important thing to remember about deciding how you feel about your partner's transvestism, is that first you need an insight into what makes him tick, so you can set your feelings in the context of your very personal relationship with this particular man, who happens also to be a TV.

So talk to him. Encourage him to tell you what his transvestism means to him and how it affects his feelings towards you and your children. And listen --- a lot.

Try not to be judgmental. Give him every opportunity to unburden himself. After all, what he does is neither immoral nor illegal. It is not a perversion, merely a variant of sexuality within the broad band of that which is considered 'normal'.

You may well be agreeably surprised to discover a vulnerable, sensitive soul desperately fearful, yet desperately wanting to confide in you about feelings that he has had for the greater part of his life and always repressed and hidden out of fear and misplaced guilt.

He has probably wanted to tell you for ages, but was too fearful. His 'coming out' may do a great deal for his morale, particularly if your reaction is neither dismissive nor hostile.

He has a compulsion to cross-dress: it is a deep psychological need that must be met in the interests of his health. However, that does not mean he has to do it all the time: only as much as he actually needs.

You never know, it may be that in time you will find a fascination in helping him transform and even like his alter ego.

Of course, the uncertainty about his management of his cross-dressing and his vulnerability may make you feel insecure.

Your provider and protector may suddenly be seen to have feet of clay --- but ought you project your conception of what he should be onto a person who is, like yourself, a mere mortal. Remember, his problem is guilt and fear of others refusal to accept transvestism rather than the transvestism itself.

Hasty rejection could exacerbate his problem, so put on your caring, nurturing hat and don't react too swiftly.

This unburdening of a great weight should also reassure you that his transvestism existed before you ever met, that you are in no way to blame for it and that it is not an adverse reflection on your femininity in any way.

Too many wives feel that there must be something wrong with them if their husbands have a need to cross-dress, whether they masturbate, or admit to masturbating, or not.

In fact, the problem lies not with the wife but with the husband's own sexuality. A good relationship with his wife will generally help him keep his transvestism under reasonable control: breakdown of the relationship can rapidly result in it becoming obsessive. As far as masturbating is concerned, it is widely accepted that virtually all men masturbate regularly, irrespective of whether they are TV or the state of their marital relationships. Although not so widely talked about, it should be remembered that many women masturbate regularly too: quite simply it is normal sexual behaviour.

However you discovered your man to be a TV, it is entirely up to you whether you will let this discovery ruin your relationship. If you can succeed in reassuring him at this vulnerable stage that you really do love him, then there is every chance that you can honestly face your feelings together.

By labelling a man a transvestite (or cross-dresser) we really do not tell ourselves too much about him.

There are many different types of cross-dresser, they vary, amongst other ways, in terms of the frequency of dressing, the style of dressing, the motives for doing it, the secrecy, their conceptions of themselves, whether fetishism or masturbation may be involved, their sexuality and the percentages of time they present as women.

Of course, living with a TV can involve some adjustments in lifestyle, but they may be a trivial price to pay for an otherwise excellent relationship. The shock horror of discovering your man is a TV may simply be a knee-jerk reaction triggered by received prejudices and perceived stereotypes. If you are open and honest with each other in an attempt to preserve your relationship, if you focus on its strengths rather than letting this particular problem become overwhelming, then there is every reason to expect the relationship to flourish. You will simply understand each other a little better.

He likes cross-dressing so he must be gay!

Not a bit of it. This is one of the most frequently encountered misconceptions about transvestites.

Of course there are gay TVs. And bi ones too. There are also those who are strictly heterosexual.

As far as can be ascertained the incidence of homosexuality amongst TVs is no greater than that of the whole male population.

He is a man who likes pretending to be a woman, so he must be bi-sexual?

Not necessarily. Many TVs fantasise about men making advances to them when they are cross-dressed:- but let's face it, many women have lesbian fantasies. A bit of fantasy is no problem.

However, some TVs carry the fantasy further and may be tempted by advances made, or even encourage them. Strangely enough, TVs in this category may still view themselves as strictly heterosexual --- reasoning that when in their female persona it is natural to have (or wish for) sexual relationships with males.

Clearly such conduct is liable to be highly prejudicial to a marriage. Whilst some may have such fantasies, or even experiment, for many TVs the excitement comes from emulating femininity, that quality they most admire in their partners. This emulation involves such superficial aspects of femininity as very girlie clothing, make-up etc.

This group of TVs may remain resolutely heterosexual and as faithful to their partners as any other group of men. A wife able to accept her husband's transvestism may well find her acquiescence to be enough to stop him straying or experimenting.

Of course, emulation of an admired characteristic can lead to a form of fetishism in which the clothes, make-up etc. of the ersatz female become a substitute for the real female. When this happens in a marriage, it is heading for the rocks. Few wives (or partners) can be expected to play second fiddle to the TVs cross-dressed persona!

He's not nuts! (or if he is, it's not because he's a TV)

Cross-dressing is currently deemed by Psychologists in the USA as a behaviour within the **normal** range of male sexuality. It becomes a matter of clinical concern when the cross-dressing becomes a compulsive obsession.

It is also true to say that the views of psychologists do not necessarily mirror those of the public at large.

Transvestism still tends to be widely viewed as a perversion and the transvestite as something of a figure of fun.

It's not immoral

Cross-dressing of itself is not immoral. It harms no-one and may indeed bring great relief from stresses that could otherwise cause considerable behavioural problems.

It does not have to involve deceit (although it usually does) but merely indulges a fantasy.

Of course, social pressures can lead to secrecy and deceit in an effort to hide a behaviour that is widely derided. So great may be the TV's fears that he may feel unable to confide even in his closest family, wife or partner, yet at the same time he is likely to wish them to know, understand and accept.

It's not illegal

Cross-dressing is not an offence in law in Britain. The TV need have no fear of the Police when cross-dressed and is entitled to expect the same courtesy and consideration from Police Officers as would any other law-abiding citizen. If stopped by a Police Officer, he should not attempt to hide the fact that he is cross-dressed.

The TV should take care not to put himself in situations in which his purposes may be misunderstood and give rise to a disturbance.

For example, when cross-dressed, particularly if his presentation is not quite convincing, his use of ladies toilets could cause embarrassment to other users and give rise to complaints. Clearly if he used a gents, he may be suspected of importuning.

The wise course of action, if he must use a public toilet, would be for him to seek a 'disabled toilet' that is designed for the use of men and women.

In Britain, crossdressing tends to be met my misunderstanding and ridicule, despite the fact that cross-dressers are, by and large, anxious **not** to draw attention to themselves as being male, wishing instead to be perceived as female and anxious only to be permitted to dress as they wish without let or hindrance, subject to the dictates of decency.

Whilst it is an offence for a cross-dresser, as with any other member of the public, to behave in a manner likely to cause or incite a breach of the peace, the mere act of crossdressing does not of itself constitute such cause or incitement.

Nevertheless, there are occasions when cross-dressers behave ill-advisedly and unwittingly attract unwanted attention. At such times, the cross-dresser may be jeered at or mobbed by aggressive groups of people.

When Police Officers are called to restore order, their priority should be to protect the cross-dresser from further abuse and/or the threat of violence, albeit with a warning to be more careful in the future when going about lawful business.

When confronted by someone they find embarrassing, many men react with aggression, whilst many women start to giggle nervously.

Those in positions of authority need to use considerable tact and to be aware that their manner of speech as well as body language could appear extremely threatening to a frightened and very apprehensive male caught out dressed as a woman.

Occasionally, fearful of ridicule, cross-dressers will attempt to prolong the subterfuge.

Cross-dressers involved with the Police or other authorities should admit their gender status immediately.

Nevertheless, police and other authorities should understand that if a cross-dresser does try to maintain the pretence there may be no guilty intent, rather a profound fear of discovery and the imagined consequent shame and ridicule.

It is a part of his character, not behaviour of his choosing

The need to cross-dress is not something learned but an innate characteristic It is part of the man and for all practical purposes, inseparable from him.

It is part of what makes him the person he is. It is as much part of him as his eye colour, sense of humour or his fingerprints.

He may well not want to be a TV, for it can be a very unwelcome complication in life. However, no matter how readily he can recognise the difficulties it brings, he is still under a compulsion to cross dress.

If all is going well in his life:- happy marriage, success at work, a very full life with little time to himself, he may effectively put cross-dressing on the back-burner for protracted periods. He may not do it for some years, or just very occasionally 'borrow' an item of clothing and try it on. This apparent remission should not be seen as anything other than a remission.

It is not a cure.

Nor is it a blueprint for the future.

WHAT IS A TV?

In the broadest terms, he is a cross-dresser who perceives himself as male and wishes to remain male. Beyond that, each TV is an individual and they do not all exhibit the same traits. Thus his crossdressing may be purely an aid to sexual stimulation, it may be fetishistic --- needing specific garments or fabrics or have become a largely non-sexual form of escapism, providing him with a feeling of calm and relief from stress.

TVs often point out that there is a 'male' and a 'female' aspect to every individual's character and that cross-dressing enables him to get in touch with his female aspect.

He is liable to see the 'female' aspects as being characterised by calm, gentleness, caring, tenderness and nurturing.

He may include submissiveness and lack of aggression in this list: his behaviour when cross-dressed may well indicate those qualities he holds most important.

Whatever the qualities, they enable him to escape into a character with which he feels comfortable and which is freed of his normal daily pressures and responsibilities.

Sexuality is a separate issue

He may be strictly heterosexual, gay or bisexual.

He may even consider himself rigidly heterosexual, yet be prepared to entertain sexual relationships with other males when en femme. This last type of TV may properly be viewed as a bisexual who denies his bisexuality and attempts to rationalise it as heterosexual behaviour on the basis that when presenting as female it is normal straight behaviour to have sex with males.

Whilst the incidence of homosexuality amongst TVs is believed to be in line with that across the whole male spectrum.

It would certainly be erroneous to assume all, or even most, cross-dressed males are effeminate gays. Indeed, many of them betray no evidence of any form of effeminacy in their everyday male lives, succeeding in maintaining successful marriages and work relationships within which their transvestism is unknown.

Some TVs succeed in gaining acceptance with their partners, families, work colleagues etc. having been open about their transvestism. Many TV organisations loudly protest that TVs are overwhelmingly heterosexual: but they would, wouldn't they?

If a man enjoys fantasy femininity by cross-dressing, his enjoyment is liable to be heightened by praise of his appearance. He dresses to please himself and to elicit the admiration (or simple acceptance) of others. It is a very short step to move from verbal to physical admiration, and it is very tempting for many a TV to act out the feminine role beyond the stage of cross-dressing.

Of course, there are some strictly heterosexual TVs who remain resolutely faithful to their partners. There are also over the top effeminate gay TVs who enjoy parodying female manners outrageously, love to shock the straight-laced and conventional. They can be wonderfully witty company, completely 'safe' as far as any female is concerned, yet unscrupulous hunters of men.

Some venues are the hunting ground for the inelegantly styled TFs (trannyfuckers). These are apparently straight males who are attracted to TVs. They will lavish praise, treat the target TV as if he were a woman --- and thus hold out the promise of realising the TV dream of acting out the fantasy with a real man.

Of course, these TFs are gay men of a particular type.

It is true that some women find TVs exciting, enjoy going to TV venues and being part of the transgender scene, for there is a thriving subculture that varies from the curiously genteel to the seedy. It is interesting to observe that such women are seldom the partners of TVs.

A few prtners of TVs do seem able to combine a relationship with extensive involvement in the scene. They may go out shopping together as two girls and share interests in fashions, make-up etc.

Before considering embarking on such a step, we would advise any partner to carefully consider whether this is a desperation move to hang onto your man at all costs and whether it reflects your own insecurities rather than an honest desire to participate in the TV scene.

Many partners accept it on sufferance: going along to TV venues, attending TV holidays etc., but obviously ill at ease and trying to make the best of a bad job. Partnership should not involve having to go through such an ordeal. Do it if you will, but be sure it is bacause you choose to, not because you are coerced into doing it for the sake of a peaceful life.

A TV is for ever – probably
His transvestism may well be but a small part of his life. Nevertheless, it is a part and no matter how great his intentions, no matter how openly he destroys his clothes and make-up, it is more than likely that he will revert. Very few TVs stop cross-dressing. Most, if put under pressure, will continue in the utmost secrecy.

They may remain firmly in the closet or resort to paying a dressing service where they can borrow clothes and cross-dress for an hour or two.

For practical purposes it is best to assume that once a TV, always a TV.

COPING WITH A TV PARTNER
You may not like transvestism, but if it is a minor part of the personality of someone you truly love, then perhaps it is worth considering making an allowance.

We have observed that in cases where husbands are forced to promise to give it up, their marriages tend to suffer because of the extra stresses being imposed upon them.

The result is that an occasional (and known) behaviour may become a secret compulsion. If it is possible to establish a way of openly coping with his transvestism so your partner does not feel pressured, then he will be far less likely to feel stressed and thus to feel the need to cross-dress.

Agreeing terms and conditions
Because cross-dressing can be a helpful method for gaining stress-relief for a surprisingly large number of men, there is a tendency for them to take advantage of every opportunity that presents itself.

If you are compliant enough, you could find the dressing becoming a regular occurrence:- he comes from work, has a shower and gets cross-dressed.

Unless you have the patience of a

Saint, the chances are that you can put up with occasional cross-dressing but not so readily with a partner who never seems to relish the conventional role of man, husband and provider.

You married a man, not a make-believe woman. Unless he is prepared to respect that fact, your relationship is going nowhere. As a working guide we recommend that together you set the ground rules within which you will accept the transvestism. These may be for example:

- not in front of the children.
- not in public.
- once only every 2 weeks.
- not in bed.

This is not a recommended list, merely an example of how ground rules can be set.

It is important that the rules be mutually acceptable. Imposed conditions are likely to be resented and may well be circumvented. Agreed ground rules stand a far better chance of being adhered to. This is a matter for negotiation not imposition.

Demanding that he promise never to cross-dress again, whether as a simple demand or a pre-condition to continuing the relationship, is pointless. He may not want to be a cross-dresser – he simply has a compulsion to cross-dress.

Like an alcoholic (or a smoker) he may promise to give up. He may even be able to keep that promise for a while. However, the compelling urge will occur again, possibly when he is stressed and at a time when he has the opportunity. He will most probably give in to his urges – it's his nature – and then feel compelled to deceive and thus begin a new round of guilt and continuing deception.

TVs frequently adopt a female name for their 'femme' persona. When he is in that role, it is generally appropriate to use his chosen female name: he will read this small gesture as symbolising your understanding of his needs. Indeed, it may help you to accept that he does have a feminine side to his nature and to give that side recognition by using 'her' name and the feminine pronouns when talking of 'her'.

Sex and the TV

It is not uncommon for TVs to wish to have sex when cross-dressed. As a further refinement they may wish to adopt a submissive role, imagining themselves as being at the receiving end of penetrative sex. If you can cope with and enjoy such fantasising you may make him very happy and find his love making far better than before. However, he should neither expect nor demand sex in this way.

If it's OK for you both --- no problem. If it's not OK for you then don't agree to it. If that causes him a problem, then his transvestism has got out of control and he needs psychosexual counselling!

There is another aspect to transvestite sex: masturbatory fantasising. Most TVs admit to getting aroused by their cross-dressing (ask yourself why they do it if they do not admit to getting aroused!).

The cause of arousal varies by individual: for some it may be the feel of nylon, for others the general effect when fully cross-dressed. Some may favour particular styles of clothing --- waitress, nurse, maid, little girl, bride etc., or particular fabrics (rubber, silk or nylon).

Typically, once they have relieved themselves by ejaculating, they tend to want to get out of their 'femme' clothes as quickly as possible and change back to their normal male presentation. Masturbation is not by any means an exclusively male habit, and is certainly not restricted to TVs.

Why did he get married and have a family?
He probably thought his transvestism was a passing phase, a sort of delayed adolescent characteristic that would disappear thanks to marriage and the arrival of children. Strangely enough, transvestism often goes on the back-burner for a while following major lifestyle changes —— marriage, a new job, arrival of children.

He doesn't want to be a woman
The transvestite may well hold women in high esteem and particularly value such perceived feminine attributes as caring, gentleness, consideration, kindness etc.

His identification with these objects of his adulation is very much a product of his male sex drive and is realised by his need to identify with women by symbolically wearing the apparel appropriate to them.

He knows he is not female, but likes to pretend to be so on occasions, even to the extent of using a female name. Interestingly, the very act of cross-dressing frequently affects behaviour to the extent that a man wearing a dress is far less likely to demonstrate aggression than he would when presenting in his normal mode.

The whole business of cross-dressing may serve another purpose too:- it gives him the opportunity to escape from the stess-making realities of his everyday world into a fantasy 'feminine' world of pretty clothes, make-up, jewellery, perfume etc.

WHY DO TVS DRESS LIKE TARTS?

It is strange, but true, that a great many TVs will cross-dress in styles that they would consider totally unsuitable for their female partners. Indeed, the partner probably wouldn't be seen dead in 6" stiletto heels, fishnet tights and micro-mini skirts. She certainly wouldn't dream of being seen plastered with make-up. But to the TV the pleasure comes from the dream not the reality. He may see a mess in the mirror --- but he imagines a gorgeous sexy young woman even if the reality is an overweight, balding man well past middle age!

For him, much of the pleasure comes from long fragrant baths, putting on make-up, getting dressed and feeling the fabric --- indeed for a good few TVs the special buzz comes from the type of clothes:- perhaps teenage female fashions of their youth, uniforms, the feel of nylon (particularly among undies wearers) or the feel of specific materials such as rubber or leather.

They are typically more concerned with the superficials of 'femaleness' --- the shoes, the clothes, the make-up --- rather than the substance of what life is like for the majority of women:- cooking, cleaning, ironing, washing, food shopping, cleaning up after everyone else, tending to the sick, coping with the mess left by pets, treating family ailments, complaints and neuroses.

That lot they will leave severely alone for the most part.

When dressed they may make symbolic gestures towards some of the more acceptable (to them) of these things (the 'girly' ones) and thus help with washing up for example, or even flounce around waving a feather flick in a vague pretence at housework!

A TRANSVESTITE IN THE FAMILY:

The discovery that a loved family member indulges in behaviour widely seen as aberrant can cause enormous stresses on account of fear of discovery with the concomitant fear of what other people would think (of the individual and of the family); the fear of being embarrassed by being seen with someone obviously cross-dressed; the worry that it may affect the children both in terms of their standing with their contemporaries and their individual psycho-sexual development; the fear that it might indicate homosexual or bisexual preferences; the wife's feelings that it indicates some inadequacy on her part as a wife; the fear that the cross-dressing may be the first step towards seeking a sex change.

Such unexpected behaviour can strike at the roots of familial security, thus frequently provoking the cross-dresser's partner into a strong adverse reaction.

Problems for the female partner

Within the domestic framework, transvestism can give rise to considerable marital stresses (many arising from deep-rooted fears) and may be cited as unreasonable behaviour in suing for divorce. A woman, upon discovering her husband cross-dresses, may well feel deeply hurt that her partner did not trust her enough to reveal his secret. That in itself is a significant threat to a relationship. In fairness to him, his secrecy may be well-founded, for he may be aware of her attitude to transvestism having 'sounded her out' discreetly on various pretexts in the past.

His secrecy may also be the direct result of guilt arising from his own experiences and upbringing: many TVs seem convinced that only they feel the way they do; that it is wrong and a perversion.

So whilst transvestism can be ruinous to some marriages, for some others it can provide a forum for a more adventurous sex life, encourage a husband to share in the pleasures of clothes shopping, buying make-up etc. (and to be able to discuss fashion, beauty, style etc.) in a way few men can. The choice to accept or reject is the partner's, but with that choice comes the obligation to ask questions, listen to the answers and try to clear the mind of possibly ill-founded preconceptions.

Are the fears justified? They can be. Fear of what others may think is a problem only so long as an individual allows his/her conduct or attitudes to be governed or dictated by the conduct or attitudes of others.

If a family is accepting and understanding, it is often the case that friends and neighbours will be far more relaxed about the situation than would otherwise be expected. After all, a family at ease with transvestism and a TV able to control it, do not raise issues of loyalty for there are no conflicting sides.

One of the problems with transvestism is that a TV may look in the mirror and see in his reflection the woman of his fantasies. The rest of the world may see a grotesque parody. It is important that he should develop a sense of reality so that he does not venture out when or if likely to cause

embarrassment to others or to draw unwanted attention to himself.
Transvestism can become obsessive. So much so that some TVs end up with far more extensive wardrobes than their female partners', will only go out to TV venues, insist on being 'dressed' at every opportunity and even engage in sex only when dressed. Under control it can be a quite harmless character quirk: out of control it can totally destroy the most intimate of relationships.

Perhaps the most soul-destroying aspect of a partner's transvestism is that it may seem to strike at the core of the relationship. A girlfriend or wife can often cope better with a female rival than either a male rival or her man who dresses as a woman for apparent sexual and other gratification. She tortures herself with doubts about her own femininity; about where she has gone wrong in the relationship; about what is missing in her that the partner has to replace by this behaviour. She sees a man presenting as a travesty of a woman and yet believes she cannot compete with him as 'her'.

So, what is she to do?

Quite simply the first thing should be for her to remember that he was a TV before she ever met him. It was not her fault. If she handed him sex on a plate ten times a day, he would simply get tired out: it wouldn't stop him being a TV in the long run.

She could adopt the "If you can't beat 'em, join 'em" strategy and go along with her partner's cross-dressing: attending TV venues, holiday breaks, parties, soirees and clubbing.

She could dress in similar style to her man:- little girl, tart, latex or whatever. As with most things in life, there are upsides and downsides to such a course of action. She may gain a surprisingly active social life. Sadly, that does not necessarily mean that the social life is entirely satisfactory. After all, it is somewhat disconcerting to take the trouble to get all dolled up for a party only to find yourself virtually ignored whilst your husband/boyfriend is being told how lovely he looks, commended on his hair and make up, complimented on his outfit and being praised for his femininity.

And what if he seems to respond to this flattery? How would you feel at the sight of him simpering with shy pleasure? And what if some other TV comes onto him --- and he does not react unfavourably?

You fear losing your partner --- so perhaps the wise action is to tread a more cautious course than the one outlined above.

If you so indulge your partner that he can cross-dress as often as he wants and so arranges your social life that it is completely dominated by his transvestism, then you have stopped attempting to compete and have given in. You have let him run your relationship completely on his own terms.

However, a relationship that works involves mutuality: care and consideration each for the other; respect for each other's likes and dislikes etc.

His transvestism is not going to go away. It is thus necessary to make a choice between finding a mutually satisfactory way of coping with it or breaking the relationship.

A mutually satisfactory way can be found if the TV is prepared to control his urges to cross-dress and the partner is willing to countenance cross-dressing at agreed times without arousing feelings of guilt or shame. She may even give him a little support in terms of helping him look as passable as possible. This could involve help and advice with make-up, clothes selection etc., and can be a mature and realistic accommodation with circumstance. He should not misinterpret such limited compliance as whole-hearted acceptance.

The one needs to recognise that there is a problem that needs to be kept in check: the other that the cross-dressing is simply a small part of the character of the man you want to be with.

It is a matter of agreeing a way of life that involves neither repression nor denial. A way that permits expression of the TVs psycho-sexual needs within reasonable and mutually acceptable limits.

It is not easy to find this balance. However much leeway you give for expression of transvestism, the TV will almost certainly desire more. The trick is to find a level that limits frustration to manageable levels and that avoids the damaging effects of feelings of repression and guilt

It is vital that the modus vivendi is agreed, not imposed.

The former has a good chance of success in the long run. The latter tends to lead to apparent initial success followed by rapid realisation of failure as the TV kicks over the traces and does covertly whatsoever he wants. Sooner or later, he won't even bother about whether you discover his deceit: he will have made his choice and his partner has lost.

If you have children, you will no doubt be concerned about the effects of your partner's transvestism on them.

Problems for a male partner

The problems for a TV's male partner are somewhat different. If the TV lives permanently in role as a woman, then the gay relationship may have the convenient outward appearance of being straight, whilst providing appropriate physical expression for a gay couple.

A gay relationship in which one partner's transvestism has been kept as a secret may well be threatened upon the secret being discovered, if for no other reason than anger and resentment at the deceit (implying a lack of trust). Whilst some gay men are attracted to gay TVs, it is worth noting that many gay men prefer partners who present in an overtly masculine manner.

The effects of a parent's transvestism on his children

On the face of it, one might assume that if a child is unaware of a parent's transvestism, that there is no problem. Sadly this is not necessarily true. If the effect of keeping it secret is to build repression and guilt, then the resultant possible resentment and/or anger can be harmful to the relationship.

The effects on children are directly related to the effect on those who are their role models and influence formers as well as whether the cross-dresser is a consistently loving and caring parent.

Young children are generally more accepting of eccentric behaviour than adults, but they can be just as rejecting of it, if it is seen to be causing Mum distress.

From very early in life we are socialised (and no doubt conditioned) to recognise that there is a difference between male and female. As we grow older we become able to differentiate between forms of conduct and manners that tend to be associated with gender roles. We notice atypical conduct, without necessarily attaching any significance to it, merely noting that a particular woman has some rather mannish ways, or a particular man seems surprisingly dainty and graceful. Later still the child becomes more sexually aware and the person displaying atypical gender conduct is liable to become the object of derision. However, the Dad in dress and make-up is a very different matter. He is first and foremost a parent. To the young child that means a life support system. The child's life revolves around the parent as provider of food, shelter, love, care, company, guidance and tuition.

If he cross-dresses openly and it clearly causes no tension in Mum, then the young child will accept the dressing as 'the way it is' and not have cause for concern. But there are few such examples.

If Mum does seem tense, the child may even see this as a result of Dad attempting to usurp her role.

Mum may well be concerned that a neighbour, friend, relative or tradesman could call. What should she do? Brazen it out and pretend nothing out of the ordinary is happening? Refuse to answer the door? Hustle the husband discreetly away out of sight? Or should the dressing only be done late at night?

Once worries of this sort set in, there is liable to be tension when Dad dresses: a tension the child will sense and that cannot add to his or her sense of security.

As the child gets older there is a further complication. Cross-dressing is still not generally regarded as a perfectly normal, reasonable and appropriate form of conduct. A child that may have no problem with a cross-dressed Dad may still need to be advised not to broadcast the fact that Dad sometimes looks like a Mum! School-fellows and teachers may well not understand. Other parents may well not wish their children to associate with the children of a perceived pervert.

Of course, the social taboos become even stronger when the transvestism has further overtones such as sado-masochism, adult baby, dressing as a little girl or as an outrageous tart.

THE CROSS-DRESSING CHILD

Transvestism is a curiously two-faced creature.

For the transvestite (TV), it is a harmless compulsion --- a simple extension of his personality (or so he may well have you believe).

But for you it is a dreadful shock, however you find out about it.

You've probably asked yourself a great list of worrying questions including most (if not all) of the following:

Where did I/we go wrong?
Why he has turned out like this?
What can be done about it?
Can he be cured?
Does it mean he is gay?
Is it an illness?
Is it a mental sickness?
Is he a pervert?
Will he grow out of it?
Who else knows?
Should he see a Doctor – or a Shrink?
What would the neighbours say/think?
Is this just the tip of the iceberg – will he go all the way?
Why hadn't I/we realised it before?
Why did he hide it?

What else is he concealing?
Is this just sexual fantasy or is it something more?
What if I/we try to force him to stop?
What if I/we try to tease him out of it?
It is perfectly reasonable to attempt to confront the issue in this way, although many of the questions are little more than the natural knee-jerk reaction of a troubled parent.

However, perhaps a more practical, realistic approach is more appropriate for dealing with the problems arising from a TV son.

Transvestism is not the problem. How to deal with it is.

Where did I/we go wrong?
Why has he turned out like this?
The first thing to accept is that his transvestism is not your fault.

It has not arisen as a result of your actions. (Admittedly, there are occasional reports of boys having been brought up and socialised as girls by their parents, who go through life with a preference for presenting as female. Such cases are rare and more often the subject of transvestite fantasy than actual fact).

Since the causes are not known, it is hardly appropriate for you to shoulder the blame.

TVs come from all walks of life, from all social groups and there is no commonly observed factor concerning their backgrounds, familial or social. Whilst it is not unknown for both father and son to be TV, there is no indication that transvestism runs in families. In short, he is a TV because that's the way he is and not because of anything you have done (or not done).

What can be done about it?
Can he be cured?
Transvestism is part of his nature. It won't go away and will not be cured.

However, it is possible for TVs to keep it under control and establish a satisfactory way of living with a part of themselves that may well need to remain discrete.

He's your child, you love him and want what is best for him.

Firstly, he needs to know that you want to understand him and help him manage his transvestism.

That does not mean that you have to help him cross-dress, pretend to enjoy seeing him dressed up and made up, offer him advice on deportment, clothes etc.

It is more important that you and he can discuss your feelings and be honest with one another.

If you can't bear seeing him dressed as a woman, make it clear that you are not ashamed or disgusted --- merely that you prefer seeing him as the son you know and love.

As long as he is aware that you acccept his transvestism without censure, he should have little difficulty in coping with it. Similarly, you must be prepared to give him the time and space to cross-dress, else you risk creating the impression that you are setting obstacles because you disapprove. There is a world of difference between approving, accepting and disapproving: the wise parent is normally the accepting one. The unfortunate truth is that he cannot be cured. All sorts of methods have been tried, including horrific aversion therapy, but to no avail. He will dress when he feels the need or the urge, and his tendency to dress will probably increase in direct proportion to the pressure he is put under.

While a son is living under your roof and subsidised by you, then you are entitled to insist upon agreed ground

rules regarding his conduct.
Older, independent TVs cannot be controlled in the same way, but you can still agree over what is acceptable to you in your home, or when visiting or going out with them.

Does it mean he is gay?
Is it an illness?
Is it a mental sickness?
Is he a pervert?
Will he grow out of it?

It is not an illness in terms of being a curable malady, nor is it a mental illness. It is perhaps better described as a psycho-sexual condition within the normal spectrum of male sexuality as long as it is kept under control.
He is not, therefore, a pervert.
However, he does exhibit a behaviour that is generally considered risible and somewhat peculiar. He will not grow out of it, but may well pass through phases during which he claims to have rejected transvestism and does not cross-dress for a while. At such times, he may destroy all his female garb and dispose of his make-up, wigs etc.
However, it is a racing certainty that he will start again, build a new wardrobe and create yet another personal image of his fantasy female.
Of course, he may be gay. It seems that TVs are as liable to be gay as non-TVs. He could also be bi-sexual. Indeed, it is not uncommon for a TV to vehemently protest that he is strictly heterosexual *"except when I am dressed"*.
Transvestism expresses itself in many different ways and seems to follow something of a progressive path.
It may well start with the boy masturbating over pictures of women's clothes in which they fantasise about wearing them and looking pretty.
Eventually they will try items of clothing (probably rustled from Mum or a Sister in the first place) and get a thrill from the feel of it.
The next step is to start buying clothes and make up, putting it on covertly. Some elect to go for normal clothing, some for fetish gear:- their need for sexual stimulation is effectively the same though. Arousal may be quite rapid at this stage and will involve feelings of great guilt upon ejaculation, at which point the TV cannot revert to his male persona quickly enough.
He is a young man with an active sex drive. If he gets a girlfriend his transvestism may slide onto the back-burner and be suppressed for a while, but not necessarily.
Siblings often indulge in a bit of cross dressing. This is normal role play and part of normal growing up. The general trend is for little boys to object to taking little girl roles and little girls to accept either, but with a tendency to adopt the female roles.
Persistent crossdressing in pre-pubertal children should be treated without condemnation (try not to create guilt) but without encouragement either. It could possibly indicate gender identity uncertainties, which, if never resolved, could indicate transsexualism.
Responding without condemnation or sign of disapproval is very difficult. The child most probably feels that cross-dressing (as opposed to simple role play) is something he is not supposed to do and therefore is pre-conditioned to a guilt response before you react.
Perhaps a little lateral thinking would be helpful here. If he has been caught secretly dressed in your, or a sister's clothes for example, then the objection is to his having used these items without asking.
It may also be worth pointing out that

whilst the clothes themselves are quite nice, they don't quite fit or are not the ideal colour for him. It is also worth getting over the idea that one's clothes are really quite personal things that are not normally lent or borrowed.

Of course, if he then asks to borrow, or asks for items of his own, then it may well be worth getting something fairly basic to defuse the demand. For example, a simple range of school uniform type items could do the trick. A blouse is not totally unlike a shirt. Boys and girls jumpers are not so different. Socks and sandals are pretty much the same. A simple pair of knickers and a simple skirt would complete the look. You have not made him feel guilty, disgusting or perverted. You have not made a great issue of making him terribly girly. You've simply made some everyday items of girls' wear available for him to wear at such times as he wishes.

It is likely that he will only cross-dress when he feels safe. He will most probably not do it in front of strangers, but has not been so loaded with guilt that he must hide his habit from his immediate family.

In the majority of cases the onset of puberty triggers major hormonal release and consequent physical change. The uncertainties tend to become resolved and the child develops along the expected lines.

Some of them will continue to derive pleasure (an element of which is likely to be sexual) from continued cross-dressing. These are the TVs. A few amongst them may later come to realise that transvestism was a temporary palliative measure and that they need to correct the bodies to conform to their gender self-image. These are liable to identify themselves as TSs.

Some youngsters will only exhibit TV tendencies at the onset of puberty. As a parent it is important to realise that they are TVs, not because they want to be, but because they have no choice in the matter.

In similar vein, being gay is not a matter of volition --- it is a matter of *being*.

The TV (whatever his age) has a compulsion to cross-dress and may be a much easier person to live with if that compulsion does not always have to be repressed.

Admittedly a few are incipient TSs and will eventually consider gender reassignment.

Mixing with others --- the TV scene

Because transvestism can be a very isolating, guilt-ridden pursuit, most TVs derive great comfort from finding they are not the only TV in the world. The result has been the gradual development of a TV scene, a sub-culture with many different facets. There are support groups (TransLiving International is a good example) that exist to provide contacts amongst like-minded people, advice and a wide range of support ranging from provision of safe venues for meetings and publication of information to access to specialised shoes, clothing, make-up etc.

They take the view that there is no point in trying to effect a cure, but very good reason for helping the TV to project his 'femme' image as effectively as possible on the assumption that if he wants to go out and about, he will need some support if he is not to look ridiculous.

It really is quite an important issue: his personal safety could depend on his having a socially acceptable appearance.

Of course, there are some TVs who can present themselves remarkably well as women. But the majority do need information on appropriate techniques. For example, the male beard is a rather obvious gender indicator. In order to achieve a realistic simulation of a stubble free female face, it is frequently necessary for males to use specially formulated make-up of a type designed to conceal significant skin blemishes. To alter the chest shape to simulate a bust does need something rather better than a pair of rolled up socks. Breast forms are available at a range of prices: the groups can put the TV in touch with suppliers who can furnish their needs without causing them embarrassment.

The groups can help with advice on grooming, make-up, with procuring jewellery (large size rings, longer than standard necklaces etc.) and help with choosing, ordering, keeping and styling wigs.

The social contacts made by the TV through such groups will enable him to share information with other TVs with similar tastes. For example, there are some who particularly favour bridal wear. They will discuss different suppliers and find comfort in discussing their shared interest with other guys.

Admittedly, this social contact can easily lead the TV to discover other venues and activities.

They will learn about other groups, clubs and venues. A terribly daring once a month visit to a secret venue might soon develop into regular trips to different clubs and even weekends or weeks away at cross-dresser breaks and holidays.

Exposure to others is also liable to help them do a better job of cross-dressing on a purely aesthetic level:- they may learn better make-up techniques and learn the dos and don'ts of trying to look, move and sound like a woman.

How do I know he is not a transsexual?

In general terms it is a pretty safe bet that he is not. There's not many of them and they are not simply rather more advanced transvestites. Gender reassignment (sex change) is not the goal of the TV --- he's usually far too fond of his hanging bits to think the unthinkable thought of having them lopped off.

TV FANTASIES AND THEIR POSSIBLE EFFECTS AND COMPLICATIONS

Admittedly some TVs may fantasise about being female, having a breast or even a vagina --- but for the TV it is no more than sexual fantasy, the subject of a wet dream rather than an aspirational goal.

There is one cautionary note that should be struck here. The TV is well aware that he is male, but irrespective of whether he is gay, straight or bisexual, he will most probably be susceptible to flattery from a sexually predatory male when cross-dressed and thus be at his most vulnerable to any sexual experimentation.

Indeed, many protest quite vehemently that they are straight and only go with a man when 'en femme' (presenting in their feminine persona).

The phenomenon of male gender confusion is difficult to explain or to understand. It can present in a variety of ways but when expressed rather than repressed, is unlikely to result in aggressive behaviour. After all, a man caught in a dress is hardly in a position to play the macho male!

Far more worrying is the effect on the average male of discovering that the bird he fancied was nothing of the sort! Some men do react with aggression if they find themselves getting aroused by someone who turns out to be a TV. They may well feel angry at having been cheated or at being put into a potentially compromising situation with another male. If a man feels aroused having known the object of arousal is really a man, the aggression may be caused through his anxieties about his own sexuality.

TVs typically report feeling at ease with themselves, calm and free of stress when cross-dressed.

TSs present as women because that is precisely what they are in the mind:- only the body needs to be brought into line.

However, there is a problem.

It is a pretty safe bet that a transsexual will have been through a TV phase, or, to put it another way, that some TVs will eventually come to realise that transvestism is an inadequate palliative measure and they need something more in order to realise their true gender identity. Transsexuals (TSs) will typically have had a long term awareness that they have a mismatch between the sex they clearly are physically, and the one they should be. There is a major difference between such an awareness and the TVs fantasies about having sex as a woman, being dressed as a woman, having a vagina or having breasts.

The TV in the workplace

There should really be no problem for the majority of TVs, for they confine their transvestism to their own time. However, it is sometimes the case that their transvestism becomes known to workmates or employers and the consequences can be unfortunate.

A TV can become the object of ridicule in an unacceptable form of bullying. He may reasonably expect his employer to take action to ensure such bullying stops.

The employer should be careful not to discriminate against the employee simply because he is a TV.

Transvestism is not a crime. It is not morally reprehensible.

However, there are sensitive situations in which a TV may be at a profound disadvantage. For example, a teacher who is a TV is very likely to suffer jibes from his pupils and may find parents complaining that such a person should not teach their children.

There is no evidence of a linkage between paedophilia and transvestism; no correlation between child molesters and TVs; no evidence that TVs attempt to persuade others to become TVs; no reason to believe that a TV will be any better (or worse) a teacher than someone right-handed or blonde-haired. Despite their fears not being well-founded, it would be difficult for an Education Authority to leave a teacher in post in the face of concerted parental opposition. It is probable he would be offered an alternative, less sensitive posting in a new area.

To be sure, his transvestism should not constitute a cause for dismissal. However, in the real, politically incorrect, robust and sometimes ugly world, the TV can easily be the butt of ridicule to the extent of making his working life a miserable ordeal for him and adding to the pressures that make him want to cross-dress even more.

It is worth remembering that transvestism is by no means uncommon. The estimated number of TVs as a percentage of the male population is sometimes expressed as up to 30% (a figure we would think to be grossly over-stated. Nevertheless, at a far more conservative 5% guesstimate, the overall numbers are considerable).

They come from all walks of life. There are TVs in the military, amongst bikers, within the clergy, the law, the police, the prison service, TV businessmen, mechanics, airline pilots, postmen, engineers and scientists.

In fact, the list is as long as the different occupations available.

The point of emphasising the perhaps surprisingly high incidence of transvestism within the community is simply that it has nothing whatsoever to do with efficiency at work.

To humiliate a TV may well constitute a hate crime. To discriminate against him on the basis of his transvestism is very likely to be illegal, and almost certainly bad practice.

That said, it is not unreasonable to expect an employee presenting as a man, and identifying as a man, to dress accordingly.

It would be quite understandable were an airline to object if a male pilot could be seen by his passengers to be wearing a bra under his uniform shirt. If the TV restricts his cross-dressing to his own time, there is little reason for his employer to be concerned about it. If he blatantly cross-dresses at work, depending on the situation, there may be reasonable cause for concern. In such cases, the employer, union representative and employee should agree an appropriate dress code. This may be simply an agreement that the TVs presentation should be male or slightly ambiguous rather than overtly female.

This sort of accommodation is often necessary for TVs who are in the process of realising that they are really TS.

They may wear women's slacks and sweaters --- but in styles and colours that men could get away with. They may grow their hair and tie it back in a pony tail. However, until they embark upon gender reassignment and identify themselves as female, it would be inappropriate for them to wear make-up, use ladies toilets etc.

Curiously enough, a glance through the back copies of many a TV magazine will reveal angry letters from TVs fulminating about how unfair it is that women can wear trousers, but they cannot wear skirts.

They tend to forget that women wear trousers cut for women and do not normally resort to stuffing rolled up socks into the crotch!

The TV wears clothes designed for women and uses artifice to attempt to simulate a female body shape:- behaviour not particularly appropriate for his standing in the workplace.

Whilst the TVs who dress completely in womens clothes are the most visible, there are many more who just wear the odd items.

Thus a TV may be satisfied to wear a pair of knickers instead of underpants, or to wear a pair of tights under his trousers and hidden by his shoes and socks.

If you assume that 15% of men indulge in a bit of transvestism from time to time (probably an overly conservative guesstimate) then there is a very good chance you know quite a few 'occasional' TVs as well as some who like to cross-dress frequently, or who habitually wear articles of womens clothing (slips, knickers or tights) hidden beneath their male apparel.

TVs and Doctors

Every now and then a GP can expect to be confronted by a worried TV wanting to know how he can stop his transvestism, or perhaps whether the act of cross-dressing means he really is a transsexual. The simple answer is that there is no magic pill that will cure a TV of his transvestism. Aversion therapy never worked (it was tried years ago much to the distress of the TVs and no doubt the frustration of their doctors).

Transvestism is not a disease, mental illness or perversion: it is a behaviour within the normal range of male behaviour.

A distraught TV needs help in understanding that he is not alone, not a pervert and simply in need of coming to terms with this aspect of his personality and establishing his own parameters for how he will let it share in his life (frequency of cross-dressing etc.)

The TV may well find the frequency of his cross-dressing varies throughout his life: his problem is not how to be prescribed something to effect a 'cure' (which he probably does not really want anyway) but to find a way of keeping his sense of proportion; a way of coping that suits his way of life and that of those near and dear to him. One further constructive course a GP can take is to recommend that the TV sees a suitably trained Counsellor (if he does not know of any, then TransLiving International may be able to help either by recommendation or via their own Counsellors).

The GP needs to listen carefully to what the TV patient is saying. After all, his problem may be rather more serious: he could be a transsexual trying to come to terms with himself. If the GP suspects this to be the case, it is prudent not to put the idea into the patient's head, for the normal strategy with TSs is to wait for them to identify themselves as TS and to seek gender reassignment.

The GP would then refer the patient to his local Consultant Psychiatrist who will, if he considers the patient to be a TS, refer him on to a specialist gender Psychiatrist.

It is important that in dealing with a man who cross-dresses, the GP should not be judgmental: "Stop being silly. Grow up and be a man. Join a rugby club!" --- not the most helpful approach, but that is precisely what one experienced GP told a worried TV whose cross-dressing was endangering his marriage.

In that situation, the GP's task should have been to help the TV understand his wife's anxieties and fears; and the wife to understand the husband's cross dressing and his fears and his guilt.

- and Ministers of Religion, Therapists and Counsellors

Transvestism is not a crime. It is neither illegal nor immoral. It is an expression of male sexuality that is so widespread as to be considered as normal, provided that the TV is able to function normally as a man and that he has not become obsessed by the need to present as, and be perceived as a woman.

On the other hand, it is the cause of many very real problems, most of which are rooted in fear, guilt or insecurity.

Perhaps the role of the caring confidant should be to help the TV recognise the effects of his transvestism upon others and to seek to find a balance between the demands of his compulsion and the needs of those around him. He needs reassurance that he is not a pervert, but he also needs to understand that his partner needs reassurance that she (or he) is the prime object of his love.

The TV can be amazingly selfish. He may spend a small fortune on his 'femme' side whilst being neglectful of his wife. In that, he may be just like any obsessive male (such a behaviour may be observed amongst some golfers) but because of the sexual implications, his behaviour seems far more threatening. A wife is unlikely to fear a golf ball, even though she may resent how much time and money is spent around it. She has perfectly understandable cause for fearing the competition of her partner's 'female side'.

These fears need to be understood by the TV: if not, he is liable to lose his partner. The TV may need some help to see how his obsessive focus on the needs of his female side is liable to damage his relationship with his partner.

Even if he is able to balance his time and attention, his partner is likely to have had the world of their relationship shattered.

She feels she is being asked to share her man with another woman, but instead of a flesh and blood one she can confront, she must vie for her man's attention with an ephemeral fantasy creature always lurking in the background and seldom seen.

Partnership with a TV is not a sure recipe for disaster, but it does carry with it a number of potentially serious problems for a relationship.

If he can appreciate the worth of a loving relationship with another person, can give and receive trust in equal measure and is able to ensure that his transvestism is accorded far lower priority than loving and giving attention to his partner, then he will be able to establish an accord by means of which his transvestism may receive expression, albeit discreet, in an honest and open way.

The task of the counsellor or caring confidant should be to help the TV understand how his need to cross-dress is impacting upon his world: his friends, neighbours, work colleagues, family, partner, children etc.

The impact is readily apparent in the case of the TV who cross-dresses openly. However, the fear, deceit and subterfuge involved for the closet TV may have a significant impact upon his relationships without his realising it.

A TV may wish to be cross-dressed for any appointment in order to better explain the way he looks and feels. Permitting this may help him relax and talk more openly. Try not to react adversely to his appearance, but there is no reason why you should not comment in a way that would seem to him to be a helpful critique. For example, if his beard shows through his make-up, you might suggest he gets one of the special products designed to overcome this problem. Your aim is to help him establish a workable and sensible balance between the different demands for his time

THE LONELINESS OF THE SINGLE TV

The married TV may have far fewer opportunities to cross-dress than he would like.

The single one may, strangely enough, be able to indulge his 'hobby' far more frequently and yet in some ways be far more isolated.

It is often the case that the single TV will cross-dress whenever at home alone for a few hours. The preparation may take quite a time:- carefully locking all doors, closing curtains, thoroughly shaving, making-up (and correcting mistakes) -- probably using foundation, blusher, mascara, lipstick, lip gloss, nail varnish (fingers and toes).

He will have to do something with his hair (or a wig) and finally complete the dressing.

All done, he can only remain hidden away prior to removing the whole kit and caboodle, making sure there is absolutely no residual trace of make-up. He may masturbate having dressed. If so, he is liable to change back to his male presentation quite quickly.

In fact, his private hobby can imprison him in a world of fear and guilt.

He is afraid of being seen, afraid to venture abroad other than at night when, vampire-like, he may stealthily emerge from his home, carefully checking that there is nobody to see him.

Usually he will cross-dress in the privacy of his home in a furtive, secretive and seemingly pointless ritual, a rather sad exercise, harmless to others. He may long to go out into the world and see if he can 'pass' without being recognised as a man. His night-time forays are liable to be his first tentative steps in that direction. He does not realise that few women take lone 'constitutionals' along empty streets at night. He feels safe clouded in darkness: they would feel vulnerable.

Eventually he will learn of groups or clubs for TVs. He will make a first fearful contact, probably not revealing his name, possibly claiming to be enquiring for a friend.

Sooner or later he will make contact with the TV scene. It could be via a commercial dressing service which is a business catering for TVs by providing a place where they can get cross-dressed. Clothes hired for the period, an hour or two typically, and a make-up service may complete the package the TV buys into.

He may have seen an advertisement for a retail business catering for TVs. They sell a range of products specifically geared to the TV market, provide a dressing and make-over service and may even offer opportunities to book a weekend away 'as a girl'.

As he gets to meet more TVs, he will learn of other venues, TV friendly pubs and clubs, TV holiday breaks and may well commit most of his social life to TV related activities and much of his disposable income to womens clothes, make-up, shoes etc.

A few will learn to shake their guilt and be quite open about their activities. Indeed, some manage to be so up-front about it that they end up lending and borrowing clubbing outfits from female neighbours.

Twenty years ago transvestites were far less open than today. It remains true that it is still unwise for a cross-dressed male to go into certain areas, certain pubs etc. even in a town like Brighton that is noted for its 'pink triangle' a predominantly gay (and TV friendly) area.

The Village in Manchester acts as a magnet for TVs from all over the country. They are safe enough in TV venues, but they would be ill advised to venture into places they do not know and that do not publicise themselves as either for TVs or as being TV friendly.

Hormones – a cautionary note
(for more information, please see the article on hormones in the final section)
TVs are most strongly urged NOT TO PUT THEIR LIVES AT RISK by experimenting with hormones and anti-androgens.

Hormones destroy the very sex drive that makes the TV cross dress and enjoy his TV life.

Hormones don't turn a TV into a TS, or into a woman. They merely make him look a very strange sort of man and may cause the ruin of his existing relationships.

Any drug that has such a potent effect on the body is extremely powerful and should only be administered under strict medical supervision with regular monitoring and following careful screening to ensure that they are not contra-indicated.

SECTION TWO

An overview of transvestism and transsexualism would be incomplete without a glance at various types of crossdressing and anomalous gender behaviours distinguished by being given specific names.
The glossary, at the end of this book, gives brief definitions of particular terms and usages that are relevant to transgender issues.

AN OVERVIEW OF THE TRANSGENDERED AND HOW THEY PRESENT.

Cross-dressing is currently deemed by Psychologists in the USA as a behaviour within the **normal** range of male sexuality. It becomes a matter of clinical concern when the cross-dressing becomes a compulsive obsession.

In Britain, crossdressing tends to be met by misunderstanding and ridicule, despite the fact that cross-dressers are, by and large, anxious **not** to draw attention to themselves as being male, wishing instead to be perceived as female and anxious only to be permitted to dress as they wish without let or hindrance, subject to the dictates of decency.

Whilst it is an offence for a cross-dresser, as with any other member of the public, to behave in a manner likely to cause or incite a breach of the peace, the mere act of cross-dressing does not of itself constitute such cause or incitement. Nevertheless, there are occasions when cross-dressers behave ill-advisedly and unwittingly attract unwanted attention. At such times, the cross-dresser may be jeered at or mobbed by aggressive groups of people. When Police Officers are called to restore order, their priority should surely be to protect the cross-dresser from further abuse and/or the threat of violence, albeit with a warning to be more careful in the future when going about his/her lawful business.

When confronted by someone they find to be embarrassing to deal with, those in authority need to use considerable tact and to be aware that their manner of speech as well as body language could appear extremely threatening to a frightened and very apprehensive male caught out dressed as a woman.

Occasionally, fearful of ridicule, cross-dressers will attempt to prolong the subterfuge. TransLiving, like other responsible groups, advises cross-dressers involved with the police or other authorities to admit their gender status immediately. Nevertheless, if a cross-dresser does try to maintain the pretence it should be remembered that there may be no guilty intent, rather a profound fear of discovery and the imagined consequent shame and ridicule.

It is important that officers or officials remember that cross-dressing is not an offence and that the cross-dresser is entitled to expect the same courtesy and consideration from them as would any other member of the public.

The conduct of a cross-dresser can seem quite strange and perplexing to anyone who has had little or no contact with transvestites. They even have a set of expressions peculiar to themselves --- a form of jargon. The most frequently encountered terms are shown in italics in brackets:-

Whilst they are apprehensive of being spotted as male (*read*) when cross-dressed (*dressed* or *en femme*), they will push their luck by going out in public en femme. This risk-taking provides a variable mix of sexual stimulation, adrenaline-rousing excitement and fear, the conscious wish to project individual identity and the unconscious wish to be discovered in order to remove the need for future secrecy. For the TV, the ideal is to be able to go out in public and be accepted as a female (*to pass*).

The male occasional cross-dresser who wishes to remain male is a transvestite (*TV*). He may be strictly heterosexual, gay or bisexual. He may consider himself rigidly heterosexual, yet be prepared to entertain sexual relationships with other males when en femme. We contend that such TVs are properly viewed as bisexuals who deny their bisexuality and attempt to rationalise it as heterosexual behaviour on the basis that when presenting as their female selves, it is normal straight behaviour to have sex with males.

This sort of sexual adventure when cross dressed may be seen as a form of fantasy fufilment.

The incidence of homosexuality amongst TVs is probably not very different from that across the whole male spectrum and it would certainly be erroneous to assume all, or even most, cross-dressed males are effeminate gays. Indeed, many of them betray no evidence of any form of effeminacy in their everyday male lives, succeeding in maintaining successful marriages and work relationships within which their transvestism is unknown.

Some TVs succeed in gaining acceptance with their partners, families, work colleagues etc. having been open about their transvestism. It is true that some wives find TVs exciting, enjoy going to TV venues and being part of the transgender scene, for there is a thriving subculture that varies from the curiously genteel to the seedy.

However, the majority of TVs wish to be discreet and most of them, for most of the time, preserve their transvestism as a secret. It should surely remain the prerogative of the TV as to how and when he reveals his secret. Of course, there will inevitably be occasions when it is necessary to call in a wife/partner/relative to identify/care for a cross-dressed man [e.g. if he has been involved in an accident]. If the cross-dressing had been a secret, the person called in may be alarmed and shocked. Considerable tact is needed.

Similarly, if a TV has to be detained overnight for any reason, shaving facilities should be made available in the morning and the help sought of a female Officer in lending/providing sufficient foundation for the TV to be able to pass in public.

If his style of dress and overall appearance is such that he would immediately invite unwanted attention, then it would be prudent to arrange transport so he can be returned home discreetly. These simple yet considerate measures are in the interests of the TV and his family. The fear of exposure and disgrace can be so powerful as to have lead some TVs to commit suicide. They are vulnerable when cross-dressed and are surely deserving of tolerant understanding

If you are aware of the jargon and can use it appropriately, and if you follow the simple courtesy of addressing the TV as female when en femme, using her femme name and the feminine pronouns concerning her, at least when in her earshot, then you will rapidly put her at ease and allay many of her fears. If this sounds absurd, just remember that the TV is already under enormous stress and the fears of rejection, ridicule and disgrace are potentially powerful enough to induce thoughts of suicide.

The occasional or the closet TVs are probably the most at risk. But there are other categories of cross-dressers.

Full-time TVs are men who choose to live as women all the time. Many of these will adopt female names (possibly changing their name by Statutory Declaration or Deed Poll). They should freely admit their gender status, have no wish to be female and enjoy the sexual relationships that they have enjoyed all their lives, whether gay, hetero- or bisexual.

These TVs do not normally fit the stereotyped image of the short-skirted, high-heeled over made-up, bewigged pseudo tart. Their clothing tends to be more discreet and they try to blend in with other people so that they are taken as women wherever they go.

The full time TV (FTV) role can be particularly attractive to some TVs as they reach retirement, especially if they are alone.

Younger ones may choose this path with a view to earning money through prostitution, or find it appropriate if they wish to work in some aspect of the sex industry (perhaps selling to TVs). Some FTVs have grown their own breasts or had implants. Unfortunately female hormones are not difficult to obtain these days and despite the folly and danger of taking them, the temptation is too great for many FTVs.

She-males are men who have acquired secondary female characteristics through cosmetic surgery and/or hormone treatment. Typically they may live as women and have breasts. However, they also possess a full working set of male genitalia. They tend to earn their living through prostitution, appealing to both male and female clients.

Transgenderists (occasionally known as **gender transients**): the term is used by those who happily inhabit a betwixt and between world in which they variously present as the gender of their choosing. Many are physically similar to she-males. The term transgenderist may also be used variously to describe a TV who lives full time as a female but has no wish to seek gender reassignment (we prefer to use FTV for these and No-Op TS for those TSs who cannot have gender reassignment surgery despite meeting all the relevant criteria.).

As with other TVs, a transgenderist may be hetero, gay or bi. There is also the distinct possibility that she is, for all practical purposes asexual.

She may have had hormone treatment (but not necessarily).

Transgendered

This descriptor is sometimes used as a generic term embracing all categories that seem to cross or span the gender divide. Its meaning can usually be adduced from its context.

A transsexual (TS) is a person whose gender dysphoria (feeling of inappropriate gender) is so acute that he/she must take action to match sexual characteristics as closely as possible to perception of gender. They may be pre- or post-operative, male to female (M-F) or female to male (F-M). Someone accepted as transsexual by a specialist Gender Psychiatrist, normally following referral from their local Consultant Psychiatrist, is put on a course of hormone treatment and required to live for at least one year in the chosen gender role prior to being considered for corrective gender reassignment surgery (the sex change operation).

The Psychiatrist will normally provide a 'to whoever it may concern' letter explaining that the dressing in role is an essential part of the therapy. Pre-operatively the TS may, or may not, have started hormone treatment it is normally the case that hormone therapy proceeds through the real-life test.

In the case of M-F TSs, those who have been taking hormones for some months will tend to have breast development. Like she-males and TVs, pre-op TSs still retain their male organs. The big difference is that they do not want them.

For M-F TSs the surgical procedure is relatively straightforward and usually carried out in one step. Some specialists prefer to perform an orchidectomy (removal of testicles) first and complete the two-step surgical procedure with the creation of a neo-vagina using tissue from the scrotum and around the penis. Tissue from the glans, complete with sensory nerves, is resited to form a neo-clitoris.

[As a matter of interest, F-M TSs have a far more complex series of operations including a complete mastectomy, oophorectomy and hysterectomy. These remove the bits they don't want --- but they can't simply be given hormones to induce penile growth. They need plastic surgery involving removal of tissue from another part of the body (typically forearm or abdomen) if they decide to opt for the creation of a cosmetically satisfactory penis and scrotum.]

Early stage M-F TSs [i.e. before commencement of hormone therapy] may well still be living dual role existences:- being male for work and female at leisure for example. If not living full-time in their chosen gender role, they will be unlikely to have changed their name formally. To all intents and purposes they are indistinguishable from TVs at this stage and indeed, it is perfectly normal for TSs to have been through a transvestite phase in which they have tried to find a way of coping with their dysphoria prior to coming to terms with their situation.

The post-operative TS has met the criteria for gender reassignment surgery and has had the operation. Her testes have been removed and a neo-vagina formed from residual scrotal and penile tissue. Physically she is a female. She has female genitalia, breasts and general appearance. She perceives herself as female and lives accordingly. She has acquired a female identity and should be treated as a woman at all times.

Only her birth certificate reveals her former physical sexual characteristics. It is probable that the law will change in the UK to permit full legal recognition (birth certificate, National Insurance Number, Death Certificate etc.)

She is not a cross-dresser and the fact that she was once a functional male is irrelevant.

Whilst the current legal position is confused:- she can have a passport showing her new name and gender, but her NI identity has not altered and when she seeks employment with pension rights, her status is quickly likely to be discovered by a wages clerk!

If she enrols at the Job Centre, she will be put in a special category (along with ex-convicts) of people whose files cannot be accessed other than by more senior staff: a quaint way of protecting her privacy whilst drawing attention to the fact that hers is a 'sensitive' case.

She may well find prospective employers finding good reasons not to employ her, if they suspect she is TS, for many employers fear the reactions of other staff as well as customers/clients.

Summary

The phenomenon of male gender confusion is difficult to explain or to understand.

It can present in a variety of ways but when expressed rather than repressed, is unlikely to result in aggressive behaviour.

After all, a man caught in a dress is hardly in a position to play the macho male!

TVs typically report feeling at ease with themselves, calm and free of stress when dressed. TSs present as women because that is precisely what they are in the mind:- only the body needs to be brought into line. It should be clearly understood that whilst transsexualism is treated medically and surgically as a treatable psychosexual disorder, the TS is not mad, is not deluded and may well be far from stupid.

Indeed, recognising her problem and setting about taking action to alleviate it is the first step in the protracted process of curing the problem. She needs to be female, yet must let nature take the time it needs to effect the physical and emotional changes and may need to let the NHS take its time to provide the funding for her surgery. This can take many years.

Faced with potential delay, many TSs find it necessary to seek private treatment:- an expensive option particularly for someone who may have lost so much. They do not set out on their journey lightly:- they are people who feel both condemned and compelled to pursue the commitment they have made.

DISCRIMINATION ON THE GROUNDS OF GENDER DIFFERENCE

Man tends to bond with those he perceives as being like him. The result is seen in class structures, caste systems, tribal organisations and on a smaller scale in clubs: working mens, gentlemen's, golf, tennis, flying etc. The corollary of this is that he also tends to avoid those perceived as different.

Thus a golf club may seek to restrict its membership to serious golfers with the financial resources to be able to contribute to the development and maintenance of first class facilities, fearing that if it broadened its catchment, it may attract people who would not take the same care.

This is a form of discrimination based on complex criteria involving a mixture of elements which may include: class, wealth, social standing, education, residential area, religion, ethnic origin, sexuality and gender.

Adolf Hitler sought to safeguard the purity of his 'Aryan' race by purging the population of perceived lower orders.

That is a far cruder form of the same thing: discrimination.

Discrimination is not a bad thing per se. It is simply one side of choice, a form of discernment.

Thus if I choose to catch a bus bound for London, I discriminate against all buses that do not.

If an employer specifies that all candidates must have an appropriate academic qualification, he automatically discriminates against those who do not. However, when the discriminatory criterion is colour, creed, race, sexuality or gender, it is based upon an element over which the candidate has little or no control. It can occasionally be justified: it is often indefensible and, on occasion, illegal.

Gender and sex are often confused. The simple distinction between them is that sex is determined by what is between the legs; gender by what is in the head. Therein are to be found the seeds of confusion.

A person walking down the street may have the genitalia of a man but present himself as a woman, believing that he really is a female with a male body form. One passer-by may perceive the person as a woman, the next as a man in a dress and the last may not be sure one way or the other. The person 'hirself' is liable to be very nervous, highly sensitive and acutely conscious of the reactions of others. The passer-by who was not sure is liable to be embarrassed and to avoid contact. The one who saw a man in a dress may be embarrassed, irritated, angered or amused.

A person may wish to present as neither male nor female, perceiving 'hirself' as of a third gender, refusing to acknowledge gender polarity and assuming an androgynous gender identity.

This person, by adopting an unconventional approach to gender identity is liable to experience a lack of understanding and to suffer social isolation.

Gender and sex are often treated as effectively synonymous, for the two are normally congruent. Thus from a very early age we become accustomed to identifying sex/gender at a glance and responding accordingly.

Normally the two are congruent and so it is hardly surprising that we all rapidly infer sex/gender from a range of visual indicators:- body shape, facial shape, hairstyle, musculature, build, walk, posture, demeanour, clothing and accessories etc.

However, when the congruence is lacking and the visual indicators seem anomalous or confusing (typically amongst people with gender dysphoria) then the normal reaction is one of uncertain malaise that may variously develop into overt hostility, amusement, derision or disgust.

In order to understand and appreciate human diversity, we should all reflect on our own malaise and how it manifests itself when interacting with people with gender dysphoria, a recognised medical and psychiatric condition that is listed in both the World Health Organisation's Classification of Diseases and the Diagnostic and Statistical Manual of Mental Disorders of the American Psychiatric Association.

It is worth noting that there are those who deliberately affect non-congruent images:- transvestites and drag queens being the most frequently encountered exemplars, yet they may well not have gender dysphoria.

We should strive to understand the inherent risk of displaying discriminatory (prejudicial) attitudes through the simple expedient of attempting to classify people. The process of classification can only too readily cause people to be viewed in relation to perceived stereotypes: a process that may be administratively convenient but is also potentially misleading. Test this for yourself.

How do you picture a transvestite ?
Or a transsexual ?
How do you envisage a gay --- or a

lesbian ?
Do you consider a man in a dress to be a pervert?
Is he a potential danger to young girls?
Is there a link between paedophilia and transvestism?
Do you consider a woman who dresses as a man to be a lesbian?
Do you consider a man who dresses as a woman to be gay?
Do you think that people who have undergone gender reassignment are unsuitable to bring up children?
Do you think a woman who was once a man has the obligation to declare her history to all potential sexual partners? Would you think the same way of a man who was once a woman?
Do you think that transsexuals and transvestites are the probable result of a childhood in which paternal influence was slight and the child only had female role models?
Do you believe it is possible for people to have a sex change --- or do you think that gender reassignment is simply a palliative measure for people with a severe psychosexual disorder?
Are transvestites victims of a psychosexual disorder?

•

Whatever your answers to the above questions, please take time to re-examine them to discover why you think the way you do.
We can lear na great deal about our attitudes, prejudices and perceptions through reflecting in this way. After you have read through the different contributions to this book, please ask yourself the same questions once again and reflect on your answers.

•

The facts:
Most transvestites **claim** to be strictly heterosexual. The incidence of homosexuality is probably about the same as in the whole male population. The incidence of bi-sexuality appears remarkably high, with many TVs susceptible to entering into same sex liaisons when they are cross-dressed (and therefore, in their own terms, as a woman --- which makes the liaison OK in their eyes): somewhat confusingly these would generally describe themselves as heterosexual.
Transsexuals may be either pre or post operative. They may be either male to female (M>F) or female to male (F>M): the former outnumber the latter about 2:1, but the ratio is becoming steadily more even. It is widely believed that as the foetus develops in the womb, its body development and brain development, normally congruent each with the other, can on occasions develop in different ways so that an apparent male develops a male body form but female brain sex. Once born, such a child will be reared as a boy, socialised as a boy, but may well experience profound discomfort in this role.
Eventually, that child may seek gender reassignment in order to remedy the problem.
It is worth noting that post-mortem studies on M>F transsexuals have shown a particular part of their brains to be similar to female brains and unlike male brains[1].
Comparative studies on non-TS gay males showed their brains to be normal male.
The findings would suggest a physical basis for transsexualism and, not surprisingly are regularly advanced by transsexuals as the causative factor in their condition.
It is also worth noting that there are transsexuals who have been blind from

birth and have no visual stimuli on which to base their gender concepts. There is no correlation between homosexuality and transsexualism. In the early years of treatment of this disorder, one of the qualifying criteria for treatment was that the patient should have been a submissive homosexual (i.e. the one who routinely adopts the presumed feminine submissive [receiving] role). In hindsight (an unfortunate choice of word perhaps!), this would appear to have been a fundamental mistake.

Transsexualism does not imply any specific sexuality and cannot be inferred from effeminacy in a male, or a female's overtly macho manner. Indeed, many TSs have tried exceedingly hard to succeed in the gender role implied by their physical appearance – thus for example it is quite commonplace to encounter M>F TSs who have married, had families and even pursued macho careers in the armed forces, police or fire services. The newspaper correspondent who had the 'scoop of the century' worked for the Times. He went with the expedition that was the first to conquer Everest and broke the news on the coronation day of Queen Elizabeth II. Later in his career, married and with a family, he was to write the definitive travel book on Venice and, subsequently, to undergo gender reassignment. Since then, she has remained one of the nation's finest travel writers with her finely crafted articles featuring regularly in the national press.

Understanding the facts will not necessarily, in itself, overcome discriminatory behaviour. It may educate the prejudiced, but cannot be guaranteed to resolve aversion to lifestyles that you may feel you cannot countenance.

However, if you work with the public, or have contact with the transgendered you really should examine such aversions and ensure they do not affect the treatment of those with whom you are in professional contact.

It is not illegal for a person to cross dress.

It is not illegal for a person to use the toilets designated for use by the opposite sex.

It is illegal for a person to behave in a manner likely to cause a public disturbance and is also illegal to abuse or insult a person on the grounds of their race, religion, ethnicity, colour, sexuality or gender.

If a cross dresser presents to you, it is appropriate for you to address that person by the name and title he/she has assumed. If a guy in a frock likes to be called Mary-Jane, then call him Mary-Jane (it's no more of a problem than using a nickname or customary diminutive style) on a day to day basis, even though you need to use his given (official) names on official records/documentation.

Just because you prefer to be addressed by a name and personal pronouns appropriate to your sex, it should not be assumed that everyone else has, or should have the same preference. Imagine if your sex and gender were not congruent.

Be aware that members of identifiable minority groups are liable to be particularly sensitive to perceived discriminatory conduct. Ask a Black person, a Jew, someone blind, deaf or otherwise disabled, someone openly homosexual or a refugee.

Why is it that refugees are advised not to declare their status when people ask where they are from and why they are here? Transgendered people are aware of the same problem of discrimination and the specific risks of consequential behaviour towards them.

It is far from infrequent that transsexuals report repeated physical attacks and having to suffer regular verbal abuse. Transvestites who venture out in public are similarly vulnerable, as too are hermaphrodites, the intersexed and people with hormonal disturbances which affect their secondary sexual characteristics (e.g. a woman who has abnormal growth of facial hair or a man with gynaecomastia).

In general terms, once people know a transvestite's 'little secret', their attitudes towards him tend to change dramatically. TSs are well aware that once people know about their past, they get treated differently, not necessarily badly, but definitely differently. One symptom of this, frequently exhibited by well-meaning and accepting people, is the habit of asking highly personal questions that they would never dream of asking 'normal' males or females.

We should all remember not to overstep the border between legitimate friendly interest and disrespectful questioning.

Health professionals, social workers, police and other public servants amy need to question transgendered people from time to time in connection with their professional responsibilities and duties. They should always attempt to question in a tactful manner and allow ample time to build a trusting relationship.

It is important that such professionals should remember that the world would indeed be a dull place if we were all the same. Difference is not a problem but one of the key driving forces for mankind's progress. It is fine to recognise the differences, but not necessarily helpful to judge them, for what criteria do we adopt to make such judgments in a reasonable and fair manner?

It is worth noting that transsexualism is not a simple progression from transvestism. It should not be assumed that a TV wishes to undergo gender reassignment: he may well be quite happy to be a man.

It should also be remembered that whilst transsexualism is normally self-diagnosed, it is not necessarily the case that every person proffering that self-diagnosis really is transsexual. Statistically, some 80% of putative transsexuals attending one of the world's leading Gender Identity Clinics (at London's Charing Cross Hospital) will drop out of the reassignment programme before being listed for surgery.

Many a full time TV (i.e. a transgenderist) will claim to be a transsexual because he knows from experience that many people find the idea of transsexualism easier to understand than full-time transvestism. We might all do well to envisage sex and gender as far from fixed and determined. In many cases it would seem that heterosexuality is more a matter of habit than positive preference:- many TVs for example will admit to envisaging a same sex relationship with another TV or TV fancier, even if they have not yet experimented.

It is humbling (and honest) to reflect that whatever certainties we feel or admit to, we too *could* experience a (for us) atypical relationship.

Gender identity issues can become extremely complex and difficult to understand. For example:

i) a pre-op F>M has been living in role for 8 years and sincerely believes that he has always been male despite knowing he was born with, and still retains, a female anatomy.

He presents as a male, passing in this capacity undetected, has undergone hormone therapy so his voice has broken and he has ample beard growth.

He wants to have relationships with straight women, but is frustrated by knowing his body precludes this at present. He has also found himself attracted to an overtly gay male.

ii) a post-op M>F has a long-standing relationship with a TV male. They are considering setting up home together despite the fact that she has had a secret concurrent sexual relationship with a normal straight male (who did not know she was TS) and that the TV boyfriend cannot have intercourse with her (her known past seemingly presenting a barrier).

iii) a post-op M>F who is living with a (very butch) lesbian underwent surgery to provide only cosmetically appropriate genitalia (i.e. labia and a shallow vagina incapable of accepting an erect male member) as a demonstration of fidelity to her intended

iv) a married family man with a history including a divorce and affairs with women (he was strictly hetero), having come to accept and understand his transsexualism, undergoes gender reassignment. She now seeks relationships with men. Still strictly heterosexual, her sexuality has been reversed.

v) an effeminate gay male elects to undergo gender reassignment in order to become female despite not having any idea of the appearance of the female genitalia. After surgery she continues to have relationships with gay males.

vi) a young gay drag queen, believing himself transsexual, thought he should seek gender reassignment. On further consideration, he decided to remain gay, but now, wanting a child, contemplates the possibility of a relationship with a woman, possibly a lesbian who might see such an arrangement as mutually acceptable.

It is thus hardly surprising that gender identity problems can cause those experiencing them some great confusion.

Sadly for them it is difficult to get informed help.

The average GP has little or no experience of handling gender issues and will tend to refer patients to the local Consultant Psychiatrist who is equally unqualified to deal with gender dysphoria.

Specialist Gender Psychiatrists are few and far between, heavily in demand although working in a profoundly unfashionable (and thus resource-starved) speciality.

There are few gender counsellors. There are Helplines serviced by a range of voluntary and charitable organisations.

Unfortunately though, these organisations have largely developed to serve their own sectors of the potential client base: some are exclusively for transsexuals (further subdivided into those that deal exclusively with M>Fs and those dealing exclusively with F>Ms) and have little time for transvestites; some have been traditionally exclusively for TVs and are somewhat out of their depth in dealing with TSs. TransLiving International is the most prominent example of a broad spectrum voluntary organisation that seeks to help people experiencing transvestism, transsexualism and gender identity problems of all sorts, as well as those 'near and dear' and those neither near nor dear, but who are also affected by, or have professional dealings with, the transgendered. Unfortunately, it, like other organisations, is not in a position to advertise heavily and so there is no doubt that a great many people needing its support do not get it simply because of the lack of visibility of the helpers.

The need for support mechanisms cannot be understated. Many TVs spend years afflicted by guilt and fear. Many TSs are risking complete mental breakdown if their need to change over is frustrated.

Treatment is deemed a success once they have had their operation and been given a post operative check by their surgeon. There is no follow up: they are left to get on with their lives and to learn how to cope. Few GPs into whose care they go have any knowledge about the effects of cross-sex hormones on the originally male body and may thus permit continuing hormone therapy at the dangerously high pre-op levels.

TVs do not receive medical (psychiatric) treatment (for the most part they do not need it): TSs must if they are to undergo gender reassignment, for the medical profession has set itself in the position of being arbiter of the matter of who is and who is not TS.

It is mandatory for a TS to live in the chosen gender role (the so-called 'real life test') for a minimum of one year (if undergoing private sector treatment) or two years (if receiving treatment under the NHS), to be under the care of a Psychiatrist and only be referred to a Surgeon if the treating Psychiatrist and a completely independent one agree that the patient is suitable.

Whilst living the 'real life test' the TS does not receive counselling or guidance and there are no mechanisms for monitoring whether the real life test is being carried out as required.

In 1999, for the first time, Charing Cross introduced a limited number of afternoon sessions run by the different support groups to offer useful advice and help. Unfortunately that initiative was short-lived, largely one suspects because of the divergent interests being expressed by different groups all claiming to be representative.

Nevertheless, the best general help resource for transsexuals is provided by the self-help groups (TransLiving International is a fine example). They can give TSs practical information on expected side effects of hormone therapy, how to change name, best methods of beard removal, make-up, grooming and personal presentation, body language and speech patterns. Their function is to help provide the back up support, friendship and information in order to help the TS establish a satisfactory modus vivendi.

It is worth remembering that hormone therapy followed by modern surgical techniques represents a fairly new development.

The long term effects of hormone therapy and the risk factors associated with it are still not fully understood, for there have been relatively few statistically significant representative double blind clinical trials on transsexual populations.

It is an unfortunate fact that many TSs will go to great lengths to conceal their true past. This can mean that they may opt out of receiving necessary medical care if that would mean revealing their secret past. They may also develop complex constructs (fictional histories) in an attempt to 'prove' they are women born and bred.

It is thus possible that you could have dealings with a TS who claims to have borne children, claims to have a husband etc. Such transwomen are displaying a worrying behaviour that may be symptomatic of a serious mental disorder.

Gender dysphoria can be successfully treated. Indeed, success rates are often quoted as being in the order of 98% for transsexuals enabled to live their chosen gender roles thanks to the medical (hormonal) and surgical treatments.

Such 'success' must surely be questioned. The operations may be clinically successful. They are usually followed by a feeling of euphoria that typically lasts for a few months. However, if the objective of gender reassignment is to improve the quality of life, then success needs to be viewed in relation to the patient's perceived quality of life improvements, or otherwise.

You should know that many TSs find it impossible to secure employment and many fail to socialise adequately. Many become marginalised, losing social standing, family, friends and self esteem. They may be forced onto the dole and into areas of deprivation where they are liable to be especially vulnerable to abuse, both verbal and physical. These people have done no wrong. They have merely wanted, as they see it, to correct a mistake of Nature. Their marginalisation is seldom at their own behest and many become bitter and hurt by it. They want to be loved and to love someone. They have sex drives just as do other people --- and they can become as easily frustrated. Imagine the torment of a F>M TS who has had a mastectomy, whose voice has broken and who presents as an utterly convincing male. He would like to have a functional penis, but knows the procedures are hideously expensive and not particularly satisfactory. He still has a vagina and may well have had a hysterectomy. He receives regular injections of testosterone which, whilst masculinising him, also has the effect of making him extremely horny! He wants to have sex with a woman – but therein lies a problem.

If you find yourself in difficulty when dealing with someone transgendered, or having to cope with the fall-out from transvestism or transgender, please do not hesitate to contact TransLiving. Similarly, if you have contact with a person who you feel you can help by passing on the contact details for TransLiving, please do not hesitate to do so.

TransLiving International has practical experience spanning some 18 years:- a vastly experienced resource at your fingertips.

It should be strongly emphasised that the group does not promote transsexualism, transvestism or transgendered life in any way. It understands the problems that these can cause, not only to the individuals affected, but also their families, friends, colleagues and other contacts. The group exists to provide accurate information in the hope that it will encourage a wider understanding. It has the additional value of providing the transgendered, or those who think they may be, with links to others and the opportunity to make contact with people who have a shared experience. Too many rack

1. A sex difference in the human brain and its relation to transsexuality

- Jiang-Ning Zhou, Michael A Hofman, Louis JG Gooren & Dick Swaab; Graduate School Neurosciences Amsterdam, Netherlands Institute for Brain Research & Department of Endocrinology, Free University (VU) Hospital, Amsterdam. Report publish in *Nature*, Volume 378, 2 November 1995, pp 68 - 70. Article indicates many other research reports.

In summary it states:

Transsexuals feel, often from childhood, that they were born the wrong sex. What is the aetiology of transexuality? No distinctive differences in genes, gonads, genitalia or hormone levels have been found. Zhou et al., however, examine a region in the hypothalamus which is essential for sexual behaviour and is markedly smaller in women than in men. Strikingly, the region was of female size or smaller in six male-to-female transsexuals, regardless of sexual preference or hormone treatment. The result supports the hypothesis that gender identity stems from an interaction between the developing brain and sex hormones.

RECOMMENDED READING:

Sex, Gender & Sexuality, 21st Century Transformations by Dr. Tracie O'Keefe DCH, published by; Extraordinary People Press, 1B Portman Mansions, Chiltern Street, London W1M 1PX @ £13.99
ISBN 0 9529482 2 2

UNDERSTANDING INTERSEX STATES

by Melanie McMullen BSc(Hons), DipFS, MBA, A.IMGT

Introduction

Transsexualism is linked with, but distinct from, intersex conditions like Klinefelters Syndrome, Androgen Insensitivity Syndrome or congenital adrenal hyperplasia. It must be stressed that individuals with an intersex condition may experience no gender dysphoria at all and may even be unaware that they are intersex.

For others having an intersex condition, the gender dysphoria may be profound or even chronic. According to John Money as many as four per cent of people, and that means around two and a quarter million people in Britain, may well be born neither strictly male nor female but a mixture of both.

There are four ways of recognising a baby's sex: genetic sex; biological sex according to internal organs; biological sex according to external sex organs; and brain sex.

Transsexualism is largely concerned with brain sex, which does not match the body whilst being intersexed is concerned with genetic and biological differences, which may or may not match the brain sex. An intersexed person may be confused as to what sex or gender they really are and feel inadequate and ashamed about their body. On the other hand they may feel trapped in the wrong body like the transsexual or they may have a dual or cross gender identity as a result of their biological or genetic ambiguity.

It is the final pair of chromosomes that makes the difference between a girl and a boy. To quote from Brain Sex by

Anne Moir and David Jessel, "if a female foetus, genetically XX, is exposed to male hormones, the baby is born looking like a normal male. If a male foetus, genetically XY, is deprived of male hormones, the baby is born looking like a normal female". The degree of extra or deficient hormones can affect whether the child is merely looking like the opposite sex or whether the endocrine system (the glands that produce hormones) and even the brain will be affected. It is not uncommon for people to be physically one sex while mentally the opposite. Anne Fausto-Sterling, a geneticist at Brown University in the USA, splits intersexuals into roughly three categories: the true hermaphrodites who possess both testes and ovaries; the male pseudo-hermaphrodites (or mems) who have testes and some aspects of female genitalia; and the female pseudo-hermaphrodites (ferms) who have ovaries and some aspects of male genitalia. She also states that "biologically speaking, there are many graduations running from female to male; depending on how one calls the shots, one can argue that along the spectrum lie at least five sexes - perhaps more".

From the earliest years, boys and girls are taught and encouraged to have different forms of behaviour, expected to place importance on different things, to act and speak differently, and to operate in different social roles. It is this whole order that is upset when there is a diagnosis of intersexuality. This may result in the person doubting who he or she is. This is because intersex states may not be discovered at birth and may only come to light during puberty when a boy starts to grow breasts or a girl fails to menstruate. Some people will go through life without realising that they are intersex. For some intersexes, they may have been aware of differences with their peers from the age of four or five, whilst for many it is at puberty that the intersex condition unveils itself. The confusion during puberty where a boy begins to develop breasts or a girl suddenly finds that her testes descend from her body is very real. This confusion during puberty and afterwards can be profound where the boy or girl suddenly begins to doubt what they are.

Take the case of a girl who thought she was a girl, but couldn't work out how she could be a girl when she had a penis! She never went swimming or took off her clothes; she became totally introverted and confused. The other kids knew something was wrong and one day pinned her down in the playground and pulled down her knickers. She said, " I'll never forget the anguish - I felt like a monster". Again a woman born genetically female but with elements of intersexuality grew a beard and moustache at 17 but doctors spent so long researching her that she almost came to the point of suicide. Another intersexual who had been brought up as a woman discovered only as an adult that she had testes and was, in fact, genetically male. He requested an operation to have the testes descended but was refused and, tragically, subsequently died of testicular cancer.

Androgen Insensitivity Syndrome
There are girls that look like girls but who are in fact genetically male. This is the Androgen Insensitivity Syndrome where the X chromosome is defective which means that although

the girl looks like any other girl she has no ovaries, womb or fallopian tubes and will never have periods or be able to bear children.

Such girls will require hormone replacement therapy that must continue for the rest of their lives, as they will not produce female hormones. An AIS woman is legally female whilst genetically male.

Take the case of Jackie Burrows whose daughter Claire was diagnosed as AIS. They first found out about Claire's condition when she was 10 months old when she was changing her nappy and spotted an egg-sized lump on her groin.

She went to her GP who referred her on to a consultant at the local hospital where he told me it was likely to be a misplaced ovary. A week later they went back to hospital and the consultant told them that upon further tests it was revealed that the tissue they had taken from her was in fact testicular and not ovarian.

She sat in stunned silence whilst AIS was explained to her and that Claire although she looked like a little girl, was genetically male. She will require hormone replacement therapy at puberty and possibly surgery at 16. Claire is, however, legally female. Her mother wants Claire to feel confident as a woman and thinks that there is more to that than genes or chromosomes.

Five-Alpha Reductase Deficiency
Take the case of Gary whose parents thought that they had got a baby girl who was registered as a girl named Alison. The baby had an enlarged clitoris and the doctor wanted further tests to be carried out which confirmed that their baby was genetically a boy as they had found testicular tissue and no womb. On the outside there was no sign of testicles or scrotum and that he was very underdeveloped and that is what caused the confusion. The Smiths were given two options. "We were told that we could give the baby a sex change and bring him up as a girl which would have been easier for us as we had told everyone that we had a girl. Alternatively, we could bring him up as a boy, which in the long run would be easier for him. The birth certificate was corrected from female to male six months later using the special statutory declaration from the consultant at the Wolverhampton Royal Hospital. Julia Smith comments that, "what destroyed me was coming home from the hospital and seeing all the cards congratulating me in my baby daughter". Most mothers keep things like that - but I burned them all".

Julia Smith felt she could not talk to anyone. Gary knew he was different but he didn't wonder about it too much as the only times it caused embarrassment were when he went swimming or was changing. When he was 11, doctors began to put pressure on his parents for him to have a sex change on the basis that Gary had been wrongly diagnosed and that he would start to grow breasts at puberty. Five-Alpha Reductase is the enzyme, which promotes the growth of external sex organs in boys before birth. Without it they will be born looking like girls and if it's diagnosed early enough it can be treated with surgery or hormones. His parents fought against the sex change and doctors admitted three years later that they had been right all along and that Gary would not grow breasts. Gary made his way through his turbulent adolescent years and had an operation to extend his penis. He is now happy as a man in a senior sales role having also been to university. Gary is legally a man.

The Hermaphrodite
Linda Roberts is an example of a true hermaphrodite and was born in 1942 with both sets of genitalia but was registered as male as her father always wanted a son. At 8 she told her father she felt like a girl and he then beat her black and blue and never to raise the subject again. In 1996 she was close to death as, over the years, clots had been forming in her legs and lungs. The surgeon explained that she was 80% female although she looked masculine. She had no need to shave and, although she had a penis, she also had a womb, vagina and clitoris. She had been menstruating since her mid-teens but had no obvious periods because she lacked a cervix. The discharged blood was causing the clots. She was psychologically damaged, baffled as to her gender and her sexuality. She had known she was different but no doctor had discussed it with her. Unsure, she adopted the macho approach and applied to join the armed services but was rejected after a medical.

She decided she must be gay as she had tried with girls but could only just get an erection. All that felt normal was going with a man with her as a woman. Besides, she had the equipment to do almost anything. In fact she was celibate for 30 years. She did marry but it was never consummated. Her wife knew of the cross dressing and accepted that but when she fully realised the full truth of the hermaphrodism it was too much for her and they divorced.

She was admitted to the Middlesex hospital in 1996 and after a body scan they discovered that she had no cervix and told her that she was a hermaphrodite. They told her that she had three options. They could do nothing and she would die. The womb could be removed and she would become a man, or the penis could be removed and a cervix constructed. She chose to have the removal of her penis and the construction of a cervix. She is 56 and is still menstruating. Remarkably, there are no case studies of hermaphrodites to predict what is normal.

Take the case of Sarah-Jane who was born in 1957 with a XXY chromosome structure meaning that they are neither male nor female and born with both sets of genitals: one ovary and one testicle neither of which work. The possession of both an ovary and a testis is known as lateral hermaphrodism. She was registered at birth as female and called Sarah-Jane Victoria, but the names Anthony and William were added - just in case. She did not see the birth certificate until years later, so she never knew about the other names. She was a difficult, boisterous tomboy and her penils was basically like a large clitoris and she had to go to the loo as a woman. She became interested in boys at 13 and didn't bother about contraceptives and thought she may have got pregnant at 16 and went to see her doctor. The doctor told her she was sterile because her womb was only partially formed. At 17 her voice got deeper and her face began to change and hair sprouted on her chin. Sensing something was wrong she went to her doctor who told her she was a hermaphrodite after having tests which showed that she had mixed chromosomes. She was devastated and felt she could not speak to her parents about it but did confide in friends with some being horrified and not knowing how to react.

At University she was sexually confused and began crossing between her two genders. Though she despised her male self, she was curious about him too. So some days she scraped back her hair and went out as Anthony William and as she was 6ft 2in, she was easily taken for a man and called 'sir'.

It did make her feel weird and physically sick. So, she sought to prove to herself that she was Sarah-Jane by growing her hair into a long mane and began modelling. She loved it and did shoots for glossy magazines. She met David through her work. There was a strong sexual attraction between them and when she told him she was hermaphrodite he replied that "no you're not, you're a woman and that's what you are going to stay".

They married in Holland in 1981 and lived together for ten years. David had affairs with other women that eventually led them to divorce in 1993.

She became ill in November 1994 with leukaemia and lost her long hair as a result of chemotherapy. She nearly went bald and with her hair went the last of her femininity.

She knew that most people would be convinced she was a man and not Sarah-Jane any more. In January 1996 the leukaemia went into remission. She feels more optimistic about herself and is having an operation to remove her male parts and make her more feminine again.

She is praying that her hair will regrow as now it breaks off when it is a couple of inches long. With her short hair people discriminate against her and have called her a freak. All she wants is for people to accept her as the woman she is. Sarah-Jane is legally a woman.

Klinefelters Syndrome
These persons have an XXY or XXXY mosaic, and Money in 1986 referred to the instability of the nervous system, sometimes retardation, and in others super intelligence, but there has been insufficient studies of this group that have been carried out to substantiate this hypothesis.

Klinefelters Syndrome does have a number of distinguishing features. These include being tall, a tendency to obesity, rounded shoulders, soft skin and face, a soft voice, no Adam's apple and also possibly breasts.

This syndrome occurs in about 1 in 1000 male births but will vary from individual to individual in intensity and the degree of ambiguity.

Some may have wombs, some may be infertile, and others impotent and more herpmaphroditic in body structure in that they may have ovotestes that produce eggs and sperm; such tissue may need to be removed due to the possible threat of future cancers.

Take the case of Patricia who began to develop breasts at puberty and whose body started to take on a more female shape.

She had ambiguous genitalia and her parents were told that the gender problem would resolve itself in time; they decided that she should be raised as a boy so she was called Patrick.

Whilst at school she noticed that the development of breasts took place and started to realise how different she was. Her classmates who didn't understand tormented her.

She went to her GP who referred her to a specialist at the age of 24 in 1986 when Klinefelters Syndrome was diagnosed. One year later she changed her name by deed poll to Patricia and started living as a woman.

In 1994 she sought GRS and this was performed at London Bridge Hospital. She still lives in rural Ireland and is still the subject of gossip.

There is then the case of Melanie who grew up as a boy and then started to cross dress at the age of 11 by putting on her mothers and sisters clothing. Later, when she was 13, by putting on a bra began to notice that she was growing breasts, which caused alarm and distress as she thought that the act of putting a bra on was the cause.

At the age of 14 she withdrew from school games by always making excuses, as she did not want other boys to see her body.

She was bullied for a time but being a tall boy she fought back and was left alone. She felt she did not belong and did not want to behave as other boys and had no interest in football or other male pastimes.

At 15 she began to drink a lot of water and feel unwell. After a visit to her GP sugar was discovered in her urine and diabetes was suspected. The tests showed that the diabetes was being caused not by lack of insulin but by profound sex and growth hormonal imbalances going on during puberty. It was thought that the imbalance would correct itself and the diabetes disappeared.

The confusion, guilt and shame continued during her school days, but she threw herself into her schoolwork and succeeded academically by leaving as the top boy of the school then went on to University.

Her voice never fully broke nor did she develop an Adam's apple although hair eventually sprouted on her face.

Unbeknown to Melanie at the time was that her mother knew of her cross-dressing but this was never discussed until many years later. Her mother thought in fact that she might be gay until there was a girlfriend at the age of 19 who also was told about the cross dressing and accepted it.

To try to manage the confusion and the sense of not belonging, she sought to split her life into the two gender identities that she had and could relate too. Whilst the cross gender identity grew stronger, she accepted herself and thought about seeking medical advice on GRS, but decided against it. She was determined to try and be the best that she could in life.

She is luckier than some in that her mother and sister accept her as well as him, and that they are able to talk about it.

She married a woman and was very happy but her wife tragically died of a brain tumour only five months after the birth of a baby daughter.

Whilst it is sometimes painful and frustrating, Melanie continues to live her life in both roles as a man and as a woman with a body that is in between male and female.

Whether this dichotomy continues or whether she will one day seek GRS is an open question.

XYY Mosaic
These are males with an extra Y chromosome, and have been cited in the press as having a propensity to be mentally unstable and aggressive with a tendency towards violence. Much of the evidence on this mosaic has come from studies on the prison population and not on the general public, making this hypothesis inconclusive.

Congenital Adrenal Hyperplasia

These are babies that are genetically female with an XX mosaic which occurs in about 1:80,000 births.

Their adrenal glands produce large amounts of hormones similar to testosterone.

At birth, the external sex organs of these children will look ambiguous, or perhaps even male, although they are genetically female, usually with developed normal ovaries.

A similar syndrome has occurred in the babies of some women who took synthetic versions of the hormone progesterone during pregnancy, which turned out to have similar effects to male hormones.

Testicular Feminisation

The development of the male external sex organs depends on the baby's body producing male hormones, especially testosterone.

Some babies who are genetically male with an XY mosaic, therefore, find that whilst their body produces normal amounts of testosterone, it does not trigger off the correct development of their external sex organs.

This syndrome occurs in about 1:50,000 births.

Whilst such children are genetically male, their appearance at birth will be female.

Their true genetic sex will not be discovered until puberty when they fail to menstruate.

Despite being unable to menstruate such children are legally female.

There is the case of Paul who was born Pauline, in that when he reached puberty, what had appeared to be a clitoris started to enlarge.

His voice started to break and his testes descended. But although Paul plays football and goes out with girls he is still, and will remain, legally female.

Turners Syndrome

About 1 in 10,000 girls are born with Turners Syndrome, in which one X chromosome is absent or imperfect, so that the ovaries do not develop, although the external sex organs are quite normal.

Take the case of Joanne Harper who longed to show off her new baby, but she couldn't because no one could tell her what sex it was.

The baby had enlarged lips like a vagina, but there was no opening and, between, was what appeared to be a penis.

They were advised to pick a name that would be suitable for a girl or a boy.

A doctor explained that Amylee had a rare chromosome abnormality called Turners mosaic that meant that the sex organs were confused.

They'd need to do tests to establish the true sex.

Then, with surgery, they'd make the child either a boy or a girl.

The uncertainty dragged on for eight months with the attendant anxiety of wondering what would happen if they make her a girl but she then grew up with a hairy chest or a deep voice!

After a further examination at eight months the doctors discovered that she not only had a uterus, but also a fully formed vagina tucked behind a sealed entrance.

She also had a single male testicle that was removed, and will need to have surgery to open the vagina and to reduce the enlarged lips and clitoris.

Amylee will also need to take hormones when she is older in order to develop breasts and won't be able to conceive because she has no ovaries.

However, she is legally a female.

Cloecal Extrophy

Joella was born as a boy, Joel. After the birth, doctors whisked away the baby as it had been born with Cloecal Extrophy, a rare genetic disorder that makes it impossible to detect the sex at birth. They could not determine the sex but after extensive tests a tiny testicle was found but there were no other sex organs. Six months later the parents were summoned to the hospital and told that Joel would never have a penis. The mother "could not bear to think of her son growing up with a disadvantage like that. It would be too much to bear physically and mentally". The mother made the difficult decision to let the doctors change her son into a daughter. The doctors said it would be easier to make Joel a girl than to bring him up as a male and at 16 months they performed the operation to reassign Joel as a girl who became Joella.

The completion of the special statutory declaration was made and a new birth certificate was issued showing that she had been registered as female at birth. Joella will never be able to have children and will require hormone therapy at puberty. Despite this Joella is legally female.

Individuals and their Parents

As to what parents can do when confronted by these conditions depends largely upon when they become aware of the problem, be it at birth or soon after, or during the child's adolescence. If it is at birth, it is likely that the parents will rely on help from the medical profession but what about if the problem comes at puberty? If parents do become aware of a situation and sense that something is wrong, they may seek to make their child conform to their expected standards of behaviour. It is in these circumstances that the cross gender identity may be pushed underground only to emerge later in adulthood.

Children do have the desire to conform, and thus to gain approval from their parents, which only reinforces this secrecy. Other parents may try to ignore the problem and hope it will go away and that the child will right itself in time. Puberty is a momentous time, but if you are intersex, this is the time you may feel unhappy that society is requiring you to behave in a particular way – one they may have felt from childhood, simply doesn't make any sense to them. For some the dysphoria may be such that they may be attracted to the socialisation process of the opposite sex.

For some intersexes the gender dysphoria may be so chronic that they will ultimately seek GRS. For example, being a person with Klinefelters Syndrome who is impotent and/or sterile may be seen as a compelling reason for them to seek GRS and live the rest of their life as a woman. For others, a cross gender identity may grow and develop in parallel if their parents are more opening minded or tolerant. As a teenager, once they are aware of the condition, it is usually secrecy which is the most common first strategy for coping. The individual may withdraw into him or herself and not participate in school games. There may well be a feeling of being ashamed and isolated with no one to talk to. There may be an intense feeling that they do not belong in this role and don't wish to behave as other boys, but may face the consequences of being bullied if they do not conform or being labelled as an oddball.

Other intersexes may be brave and individualistic and show their true behaviour, but who risk being called names like "poofter" and being bullied. Some children will succeed by putting their ambiguity at bay, and succeed academically where their behaviour is accepted as a personal idiosyncrasy. Other intersexed children may succeed by being a comedian in the sense that, whilst they are regarded by their peers as being different, they are accepted on the basis that they are a good laugh. Other intersexes may try to over-compensate for their feelings of inadequacy and try to conform by trying to be a he-man or a girlish girl. In the case of children today, they can phone Childline, and there is a Gender Identity Development Clinic at St. Georges Hospital in Tooting, London that also deals with gender identity problems in children.

Eventually, there comes a time when individuals have to confront themselves about what they are. This may mean accepting themselves for what they are, trying to make the best of their role in their sex of birth by forming relationships or even marrying. For other intersexes this may be impossible and, like the transsexual, there may be a feeling that they are trapped in the wrong body, and therefore seek gender reassignment surgery. Other intersexes may try to manage their confusion, doubts and feelings by having two gender identities, which they live and work in, and go between on a regular and consistent basis. Whilst this is a compromised lifestyle, it is in fact a gender purgatory, since they may fear that one day it is the gender identity opposite to that of their birth which may eventually dominate and which might lead to a decision on GRS.

There may also be the practical considerations to consider such as a person with Klinefelters wearing a bra to protect and support his/her breasts that is disguised under a shirt or jacket if they live or work as a man for all or part of the time. Other intersexes such as AIS women and those that have Turners Syndrome will have to take female hormones like the transsexual for the rest of their lives.

The situation with intersexes is that it does highlight a number of anomalies in that those children born with ambiguous genitalia are nevertheless assigned to one sex or the other. This generally depends on the size of the penis at birth or soon after. It has been common practice amongst doctors to operate on children to create surgical females where there is ambiguity in the genitalia at birth. Such people as they grow up may or may not identify with the gender identity of the sex they have been assigned to, and experience a great deal of distress in later life. On the other hand, some intersexes that have been conditioned to live as one particular sex and then it becomes apparent that they are not physically of that sex, may still want to carry on and define themselves as that sex. The question must be asked as to why must GRS be performed at birth some years before a child can express its own gender identity. Whilst GRS is done on intersexes, then why is it denied to transchildren.

The number of rectifications of the birth certificates that are done in the UK for intersexes using the special statutory declaration is an official secret other than it does occur. The evidence that the Registrar General will accept depends on the weight of the supporting medical evidence of the consultant, which may be inconsistent. Some who have Klinefelters Syndrome seem to succeed whilst others do not, whilst the position under Scottish Law permits rectification for Klinefelters Syndrome. It is also very hard to draw a clear distinction in the Joella case above with that of a transchild, except that rectification of the birth certificate was permitted for Joella but would not be for a transchild.

References
Endocrinology, PH Wise, Churchill (1986)
Venuses Penuses, J Money, Prometheus book, New York (1986)
Myths of Gender, A Fausto-Sterling, Basic Books, USA (1985)
Trans-x-u-all, Tracie O' Keefe and Katrina Fox, Extraordinary Peoples Press (1996)
Sex Gender & Sexuality, Dr. Tracie O'Keefe, Extraordinary Peoples Press (1999)
Understanding Gender Change, Jane Playden (1994)
The Five Sexes, New Woman October (1993)

Further information
- AIS Support Group
PO Box 269, Banbury, Oxon, OX 15 6YT
www.medhelp.org.www.ais
- Intersex Society of North America
www.isna.org/
- Klinefelters Syndrome Club UK
www.hometown.aol.com/kscuk/index.htm
- The Gender Identity Centre
Charing Cross Hospital, London W6 8RF
Telephone: 0181 846 1234 (for NHS patients)
- The London Institute for Human Sexuality
10 Warwick Road, Earls Court, London SWS 9UH
Telephone: 0171 373 0901 (for private patients).
- Gender Identity Development Clinic
St Georges Hospital, Tooting, London SW17 ORE
Telephone: 0171 686 0393 (for children)

SECTION THREE

This section is devoted to advisory articles of relevance to both transsexuals and transvestites.
Many of the issues raised are more pertinent to transsexuals and full-time transvestites, but all those who wish to cross-dress and pass satisfactorily should find much of the information useful.

COMING TO TERMS WITH YOURSELF

Perhaps the most difficult thing to do is to be totally honest with yourself in the matter of gender.

Perhaps part of the problem is rooted in the conflict between your own perceptions of your gender and those that you have been socialised to accept as appropriate to you.

Unfortunately though, the way you feel cannot always be the sole consideration.

For example, realisation that you are bisexual, or an incipient bisexual, is not sufficient justification to cheat on your existing partner.

Similarly, the fundamental belief that you are a different gender from that denoted by your sex is not reason enough to ruin the lives of others by ignoring commitments made and obligations arising therefrom.

For example, many TSs, denying to themselves that they have deep psychosexual problems and determined to try to prove themselves to be the people they are supposed to be, enter into relationships or marriages.

They surely have an obligation to their partners to disentangle the relationship in as least damaging a way as possible. Indeed, what sort of foundation for the start of a new life is the wilful and care-less destruction of an existing relationship?

What sort of foundation for the new life is guilt over the old?

Transvestites too should be aware that their compulsion to dress is at variance with socially accepted conduct.

Whilst the dressing is a harmless activity if it hurts no-one else, it can do a great deal of damage to relationships if carried out without regard to the sensibilities of others.

Indeed, whilst the TV can rationalise about his rights of self expression, the unfairness of women being able to wear trousers etc., it is a simple fact that his insistence upon dressing may be sufficient for a divorce petition citing grounds of unreasonable behaviour.

However, the key thing to establish is how you feel about yourself and your gender.

This requires absolute honesty and some searching questions about your motivations and sexuality.

Is transvestism/transsexualism an escape mechanism?

Have you ever sought other ways of escaping the pressures of your life?

By dressing like a woman, are you giving yourself permission to behave like one vis a vis men. In other words, are you attracted to men but sufficiently homophobic by upbringing to require a way of rationalising these desires?

Taking the issue of escape mechanism a stage further --- are you in danger of attempting to turn a fantasy into reality?

If you truly believe, and have always felt, that you are/should be a woman, is it likely that by effecting a change through medical and surgical intervention, your quality of life would improve? --- be honest with yourself:- it would be hard to imagine someone who presents like a heavyweight wrestler or Olympic shot putter transforming successfully.

It is worth remembering that transvestism and transsexualism only too easily become such potent forces that they take centre stage in life, pushing aside normal considerations and leading to totally selfish patterns of behaviour driven by the need to gratify the compulsion. Is it worth sacrificing the happiness and security of those people who rely on you – your family – in order to present yourself differently?

It should also be remembered that transgender getting out of control is often attributable to recent traumatic events: a bereavement or a loss of employment being typical examples.

As a general rule it is desirable that people attempt to find coping mechanisms that let them continue with the jobs for which they are trained; to sustain the relationships they have struggled to build; to maintain the standard of living to which they are accustomed; to fulfil existing commitments and obligations. However, there are those whose deep uncertainties about their gender cause such confusion that they cannot cope alone.

They need external support/s to help them come to terms with and accept their gender identity.

They need to be given the freedom to reach an understanding of themselves as part of the essential evolution of their full personalities.

Given such freedom (simply time and space free of external pressures) they can achieve success in life. Denied it, they frequently suffer depression and mental breakdown.

They are caught by a personal evolutionary force they cannot control, cannot direct and initially cannot understand.

That evolutionary force may lead them along the path of transsexualism or to a way of coping involving some physical changes.

It may express itself through full time living in a new gender role, through various extents of cross-dressing or even through adoption of a personal expression of 'third' gender, neither male nor female.

FITTING ROOM PROTOCOL

This item arose from an article by Fiona Barton that appeared some time ago in The Mail on Sunday. It concerned Debenhams' ladies fitting room policy on TVs which dictates that TVs wearing women's clothing cannot try on men's clothes in the women's changing rooms and must remain dressed as women throughout any transaction. They may also use ladies loos and try on lingerie. Sounds great — or does it?

We take a rather more robust view on this matter:

Communal fitting rooms:
Neither TVs nor pre-operative TSs should presume to use communal fitting rooms.
Women are entitled to assume co-users of such facilities are all female.
Postoperative TSs, having had gender reassignment surgery, should **normally** not be a cause of embarrassment.

Use of ladies loos and fitting rooms:
Women may, not unreasonably, feel distinctly unhappy at men trying on underwear.
Men who are obviously crossdressed are highly likely to cause women discomfiture when they are seen to be using the loos and fitting rooms provided for the use of women.

Duty of care:
A TV has the same duty of care as any other person in terms of avoiding conduct liable to precipitate a disturbance. It is thus desirable that if

he wants to try on clothes, he lets the shop assistant know of his wish and his true gender. The assistant is then able to decide to which cubicle to direct him, and to ensure that its curtains are properly closed.

Because staff in many shops are accustomed to popping their heads round fitting room curtains to check with customers that all is well, the TV (or pre-operative TS) should consider forewarning any sales staff that she would prefer not to be checked on, particularly if there is any chance at all of staff being caused embarrassment. Because living in role is a requirement of the 'real life test', completion of which is a condition precedent to gender reassignment surgery, many pre-operative TSs will expect to be able to conduct themselves in the same manner as other women. However, they should understand that no matter how they feel about it, no matter how convinced they are that they are female by gender, the evidence of their genitalia (and possibly voice) demonstrates that they are not the same as other women. Thus they should be careful to avoid causing or giving offence. If this means keeping clear of potential problem situations, then that is precisely what they should do.

Unfortunately, part of the enjoyment of transvestism is the adrenaline rush of excitement felt by the TV through going out in public dressed as a woman. Doing things that as a man he could not, enhances his pleasure. Going shopping and trying on women's clothes, testing make-up at a cosmetics counter and using a ladies toilet are examples.

He should forgo these pleasures if it is liable to cause offence to others.

For every transvestite who passes as a woman, there are dozens more who mistakenly believe they pass satisfactorily. Unfortunately, the reality for most is that their voices are give-aways, their body language wrong, their manner of walking appears somewhat incongruous and their build is suspect.

Other common errors include too much make-up, too much jewellery, heels too high, skirts too short, wrong choice of styles for age and size, wrong colour combination and poor condition wig. Many go right over the top with a look that may be very glamorous in the setting of a nightclub that welcomes exotic people, but is hardly the thing for traipsing up and down the aisles in Tesco (or even for browsing through the rails in the local Debenhams). Sadly, many of these fool themselves that they pass well. Some incline to the uncaring view that it is their business alone and it does not matter what others may think.

Shops should be aware that not all TVs (or TSs) are considerate, and that therefore staff should be free to steer them to fitting room areas where they cannot cause offence, or to point out that there are no suitable facilities. Similarly, if a particularly malodorous woman comes into a shop, the staff may well try to guide her discreetly to a fitting room well away from other customers. Perhaps they should apply the same sort of tactic to the 'iffy' as well as the 'niffy'.

Whilst most TVs and TSs oppose discrimination on grounds of race, colour, religion, sex, gender or sexuality, they should also avoid conduct that can be construed as liable to cause offence.

The simple truth is that a man in a

dress who looks like a man in a dress cannot reasonably be expected to be treated as a woman — for quite obviously he is not.

TVs and TSs should never forget that many women feel nervous of men and feel particularly vulnerable when in a state of partial undress.

Their nervousness is understandable and you should make all due allowance for it.

Less obvious perhaps is the fact that some shop staff may feel intimidated by, and very nervous of, a 'fella in a frock'. It is only simple courtesy to be pleasant, undemanding and considerate.

You know how you feel about yourself: there is no reason why they should view you in the same way.

Don't be so unreasonable as to expect or demand that other people view things the way you do. Some staff have deeply held moral or religious convictions about gender reassignment and/or about cross-dressing.

They are entitled to hold those convictions, howsoever misguided or ill-informed you may believe them to be.

Whilst they have a similar duty to yours to avoid causing a disturbance, as well as an obligation not to behave in an offensively discriminatory manner, you could well find yourself treading on some fine sensibilities:- so tread carefully and if you sense that your presence is an embarrassment, do not hesitate to back off.

After all, the fact that you are possibly going to spend some money does not confer any special rights upon you.

Store staff may quite understandably feel that other customers would be offended by someone blatantly male being allowed to try on ladies clothes. This is particularly likely in a business where you may be seen parading by younger girls.

So take care and don't presume too much. Aim to be discreet, appreciative and unfailingly courteous.

Follow these guidelines and you are likely to be welcome.

Don't and you won't.

THE FEMALE VOICE

For TVs who wish to go out in public and to pass undetected, and for TSs who wish to be accepted as women, the male voice they developed at puberty can be one of their greatest giveaways.

Few guys have the ability to talk like women: some actors and mimics can achieve it, but they are few and far between.

What makes a voice male or female?

It's partly the pitch of course. Womens' voices are, on average, set in a higher register than those of men.

It's also the intonation — the sing-song or melodic line in speech. The other factors are the vocabulary (women tend to express themselves in a different way) the accompanying body language and the resonance.

What can be done?

You can lighten your pitch to some extent. But don't try talking in a falsetto simulation of your pre-pubertal pitch: it would sound ridiculous. In general, it is advisable to lighten your pitch just a little — enough to make a difference without being uncomfortable.

Men tend to speak with far more definite inflexion rather than melodic sing-song. A man may well use three notes if you think in musical terms. The median note carries most of the words, it is relieved from time to time by the half a tone uplift at the end of sentences when wishing to denote uncertainty or a question. Statements and speech endings generally end on a descending half tone.

Women have much greater variety in their speech sound patterns.

A man's voice seems almost to emanate from his chest. A woman's from nearer the bridge of her nose. If you think of voice projection in terms of playing a musical instrument, then visualise the man's soundbox as his chest, the woman's as her head.

It is often suggested to TVs that it is possible to simulate the female voice by using a loud whisper. Actually it tends to sound rather like a man whispering, is difficult to hear and draws unwanted attention to 'why you're speaking funny'.

The other thing to watch is that you don't sound ludicrously camp. The best trick is to use a cassette recorder and experiment with different voices.

Unfortunately it is very hard to develop a 'female' voice if you keep having to switch back. In this the TV is at a profound disadvantage. TSs who live full time have the chance to cultivate their new voice and, after a somewhat uncomfortable period during which they are constantly tweaking it, most settle down to a compromise they can cope with.

Once living full-time in role, they should be able to get speech therapy on the NHS. There is little point in attempting it whilst having to use a male voice some of the time. We recommend TS ladies to go for speech therapy, albeit with no great expectations. It can be a useful help and will often assist the TS in finding the working voice that she can manage with, even though she may be aware that it is not ideal.

A few succeed in getting voices that cannot be distinguished from those of natural females and some find that singing lessons help expand their vocal register and help them to manage tone and pitch more effectively.

Most of them have voices that are a little 'iffy' at times. It is not unusual for them to find their voices serve them perfectly well on a face to face basis, but do not hold up well on the phone. Many TS ladies get quite upset at being addressed as "Sir" when making a phone call.

Indeed, such can be their distress that some find it necessary to have surgery. This is a subject that is somewhat contentious, for a surgeon cannot guarantee that the outcome will be an improvement.

The downside is a scar on the neck, which the surgeon will attempt to position to fall into a natural skin crease. Livid and swollen at the outset, it needs to be disguised with a scarf. Over the ensuing months it fades and becomes far less conspicuous. Some people tend to lose scars quite quickly. For others, they always show. It is something that needs to be taken into consideration.

The result of surgery is not going to be the production of a perfect female voice. It may make a slight difference, just a slight edge. Thus, for example, success may be measured in terms of less people taking the TS's telephone voice for that of a male.

Incidentally, let's correct two common misconceptions:

i) Female hormones will not cause the broken voice of a male to become a female voice.

ii) Having the op. will not cause the broken voice of the male either to become a female voice or to revert to its pre-pubertal sound.

On the other hand, a female to male TS does benefit from the androgenic hormones, for they cause the voice to break (and the beard to grow).
Whoever said life was fair?
It should be remembered by TSs that a fair few women also have 'iffy' voices and often get mistaken for men on the phone. But of course, because they **know** they are women, and always have been, they have nothing to hide and tend not to get so upset.
So, in short:- practice with a cassette/ tape recorder, use typically female phraseology, develop a more musical intonation, avoid chest resonance by projecting the voice from the 'mask' ---- behind the face ---- and listen to the way women express themselves through the combined use of speech, sounds and body language.
Even if you do develop a first class female speaking voice, you may find that it lacks the power of your old voice. You might once have been able to stop a tank in its tracks: your new voice is unlikely to have such carrying power, and if you force it you may be somewhat disconcerted to find the resultant tone sounds far from feminine!

PRESENTING YOURSELF

Appearance is important to us. It provides the key as to how we are first perceived and, for M to F TSs it is important that they are immediately perceived as female.
Hair, make-up and dress go a long way towards creating that desired perception, but there are other significant factors too.
Body language --- the way you use your hands, the way you walk and move, your stance --- these are powerful influences too.

Speech – the manner in which you express yourself:- your vocabulary, intonation and facial expressions whilst conversing –these too are highly significant.
There are so many factors to consider:- is our style of dress appropriate in terms of time of day/night, place and our age?
Is the make-up right for the conditions and does it effectively mask the presence of a beard? Are we walking properly, sounding right, putting out the right impression?
And it is just the very fact that there is so much to think about that can so easily catch us out.
A girl who was female born never has to worry if she looks female. She may well worry about whether she looks a mess, but she doesn't have a fundamental insecurity over gender.
The TS is only too well aware that she has a past she would prefer to hide, and the pre-op TS is particularly likely to be well aware of other little problems she needs to hide too.
The result is the oft seen habit of TSs to overdo the feminine bit – to be over expressive with the hands, to develop extravagant habits of speech, to be over made-up, to simper horrifically or simply exaggerate every characteristic they associate with female behaviour patterns. The natural born girl doesn't have to work at seeming to be female: the TS should not appear to be working at it either. The TS should be using art that conceals art
Why is it that drag queens so often stand out like sore thumbs? Their make-up is often immaculate, their wigs exquisite, they may lavish hours on getting ready to go out and spend fortunes on clothes --- but they are simply OTT --- they are parodying

women rather than living as women. Perhaps the key factor for any TS is to become comfortable in her new role in life, to feel natural and to be relaxed. One of the problems in offering guidance on matters of presentation is that it is all too easy to adopt a 'formula' approach along the lines of --- 'women walk this way ---- women talk in such and such a manner ---- women sit like this' etc.

The fact is that women don't conform precisely to any such formulae. Nevertheless, there are broad behavioural and presentational patterns typically female and patterns typically male. The task of the TS is to attempt to shift the overall balance towards female patterns.

Over the years TransLiving International has produced a range of articles and guides designed to help those pursuing gender assignment to progress through transition in as painless a way as possible. The following sections are extracted from this material:

HIDING THAT BOTHERSOME BEARD

One of the most awkward problems to beset most TVs and early stage TSs, is that of an unwanted blue shadow — the giveaway sign that even the best shave cannot totally hide. But there is an answer that has proved highly satisfactory thanks to Dermablend, an excellent product that provides complete beard cover without looking as if you have plastered on the make-up.

Quite frankly, ordinary foundation is really not 'man enough' for the job. Dermablend has been specially formulated to overcome skin discoloration problems such as those caused by birthmarks or by vitiligo, the complaint which involves loss of pigment, as well as those caused by an incipient beard.

As with other forms of make-up, there is a knack in knowing how to use it properly to ensure good cover that really lasts.

It's also important to ensure that you select the right colours.

If you live within easy reach of the TransLiving office, or can get to our parties, then we will gladly recommend the best colour for your skin tone (you can try it out of course!) and show you how to apply it.

If you live some distance away, then by all means send £1 and a **stamped addressed envelope for colour samples** to the following address:

Stacy Novak
PO Box 3
Basildon
Essex SS13 3WA

It would be helpful if you could give a broad indication of your colouring (Asian, Afro-Caribbean, Indian, Mediterranean, Anglo-Saxon) so that we can send you the appropriate selection of shades.

Once you have made your choice, it is a good idea to telephone us on 01268 583761 so that Stacy (who is, incidentally, a trained Dermablend Consultant) can explain the best way of applying your beard cover, how to fix it etc. Admittedly there is a leaflet that comes with the Dermablend, but you really want to know the best way of using the product to conceal your beard.

If you follow the leaflet you would use the sponge as an applicator — and get through the Dermablend at a rate of knots as the sponge tends to soak in far more than your skin does.

We don't think this is a particularly good idea because your cover then works out rather expensive.

Follow Stacy's technique using a finger tip and the product lasts far longer and can be applied with great control:- neither too little nor too much.

Because removal of beard cover by electrolysis can take so long, many TSs need a slightly stronger cover than conventional make-up, even if they need it only on part of the face. There is also a product ideal for this purpose.

Of course, there is the question of how to get rid of all traces of make-up too. Dermablend's Cleanser really is amazing and, correctly used, will leave you clean as a whistle.

If you would like to know more about Dermablend and how best to use it, then don't hesitate to phone. It is non-allergenic and not tested on animals. If you have electrolysis, then eventually you will need Dermablend no longer and facial shaving will become a distant memory.

STACY'S RECOMMENDED SELECTION OF BASIC BEAUTY PRODUCTS

Cleanser

Toner (dry skin)
Astringent (greasy skin)
to close pores and remove grease
Moisturiser

DERMABLEND (Available from Stacy: necessary whilst the beard shadow still shows)

Loose face powder Translucent

For those who no longer have a beard shadow, lighter foundation is used.

Those with a ruddy complexion use green toned foundation first, to tone down redness use BOOTS NO 7

Eyelash curlers, Eye lash brush and comb

Mascara

Eyelid colours and pencils. A black or brown Kohl pencil

Highlight for eyes and cheek bones

Blusher and brush

Lip liner pencil, lip brush, lipsticks

Dermablend Cleanser: excellent for removing all makeup (and gentle round the eyes)

Hand cream
Deodorant
Body moisturiser

Remember, just because you are a woman (albeit a Jenny-come-lately) it does not mean you have beautiful translucent skin. Come to that, most women don't.

But one thing you need to remember is to keep your skin well moisturised. Far too many TSs spend small fortunes on surgery in the hope that the knife will turn them into what they want to be, and neglect totally the most rudimentary care for the most crucial part of their anatomy --- the face.

Your skin is the largest organ in your body. It is the one that takes the most abuse:- weathering, shaving, electrolysis/laser treatment, waxing, plucking, and exposure to all sorts of pollutants. Small wonder that you can end up with crocodile like hide on the

face instead of soft skin.
If you need a golden rule in three key words it would have to be:
> *moisturise,*
> *moisturise and*
> *moisturise.*

I'm a woman now --- I don't need all this make-up –

Most TSs have passed through a 'tranny' stage when they managed to cope by periodic cross-dressing. Like most TVs, they would spend hours shaving, preparing, making up and dressing. A great many start on the hormones and stop bothering:-
'I'm a woman now – I don't need all this make-up'.

Sure, you may be a woman, but be real – look in the mirror and ask yourself are you really looking so very different from when you were a TV?

Could you go into a tranny venue secure in the knowledge that everybody would take you for a real girl?

Could you answer the door at 7am to the postman (before you've shaved and made up) knowing for certain that he wouldn't spot anything just a little unusual about you?

Don't overdo it, but at least make the effort to pass.

Just because a Psychiatrist has accepted that you really are a woman and should have corrective hormone therapy, doesn't mean that the world at large will see you the same way.

SECTION FOUR

*This section looks at transsexualism,
how it impacts on others,
how they can try to understand it
and some of the problems specific
to transsexuals*

A TRANSSEXUAL SON: AN INFORMAL GUIDE FOR PARENTS

Transsexualism is seldom obvious, usually kept well hidden for protracted periods and may have been disguised as transvestism for some time.

Which tends to make the revelation that your son is a transsexual (TS) an almighty shock.

However, despite claiming to be TS, it is possible he is not. For example, it is not uncommon for a young gay man to deny his homosexual tendencies --- even to himself, and prefer to believe he should be female.

What is certain however, is that your son has suffered gender identity problems and, in attempting to address them and come to terms with his sexuality and feelings of gender identity, he has come to believe that gender reassignment will resolve his difficulties.

It is possible that he may be right.

It is possible that he has a 'brainset' more in keeping with a female than a male.

It is also possible that gender reassignment would only compound his problems. He needs to understand clearly what is involved medically, surgically, cosmetically, legally, socially and financially.

He needs to see a range of other TSs to understand how their lives have been affected, how well (or badly) they have adapted and how well they function socially.

Acknowledging to himself that he is a TS would have been a major obstacle cleared. Having to come clean to you is yet another daunting one for him, and, in the process of change, he will need to clear many more.

A transvestite (TV) will dress as a woman when he wishes --- and when it is safe to do so. When he has had enough, he can undress, hide his false breasts in a drawer, remove his wig, remove his hip and bum pads (yes, a few do use them), clean off the make up and revert to his normal male self. But sooner or later, the TS must live as a woman all the time.

The TS who enters a gender reassignment programme has a daunting task ahead. She will pass simultaneously through the equivalent of puberty and menopause: breast development plus hot flushes, marked mood changes, weepiness, cramps, and many get sore nipples.

But whilst her problems are major and her need for your understanding and support great, for she is emotionally highly vulnerable, she may well appear inexplicably oblivious to the effect she has on her parents, siblings, friends and relations.

She needs to be reassured of your support and love. In return, her focus is likely to be heavily on self, she is liable to be temperamental, indiscreet and hyper sensitive. In short, you are in for a rough ride. Especially if you slip up over the use of the feminine pronoun and her name.

The initial reaction of parents to the news tends to be more or less as follows:

Where did I/we go wrong?
Why he has turned out like this?
What can be done about it?
Is it an illness and can he be cured?
Does it mean he is gay?
Is it a mental sickness?
Who should I contact?
Should he see a Doctor, a Counsellor or a Shrink?
What would the neighbours say/think?
How could he cope?

Why hadn't I/we realised it before?
Why did he hide it from me/us?
Can I/we get him to change his mind?
How can we cope: what do we tell people?
How on earth will he look?
How long will it take?
How will I feel if he brings a boyfriend home?

THE YOUNG TS

With young TSs certain other questions spring to mind:
Might he grow out of it?
Is it better to change before completion of adolescence?
What if his psyche is lagging behind his physical development --- who's to say that in five or six years time he wouldn't become a normal healthy male?
Is he simply over impressionable and identifying just too closely with a female figure?
Isn't he just too young to make up his mind over gender and sexuality?
Wouldn't it be best for him to have some experience of life before doing anything irreversible?
Could this just be attention seeking?
Who can I talk to about this?

With older TSs other problems may enter the frame:
What about his marriage; his wife; his children?
How will this affect his employment prospects?

Then there are all the practical issues:
How does he develop a female voice?
What are the risks of hormone therapy?
How does he mask/get rid of his beard?
How does he learn to act, sound, move and present himself like a woman?

How does he legally change his name?
What about passports and qualifications?
How long will it take, how much will it cost?
Who must he tell --- and when?
When should he start to live as a woman?

•

And there will be more besides. The fact is that he is not the only one needing help and support. You need it as a parent for your own sake, and to gain the necessary knowledge to be a parent who can give your TS child support.

•

Where did I/we go wrong? • *Why he has turned out like this?* • *What can be done about it?* • *Is it an illness and can he be cured?* • *Does it mean he is gay?* • *Is it a mental sickness?* • *Who should I contact?* • *Should he see a Doctor, a Counsellor or a Shrink?*

•

So your son is a TS. That's simply the way he was made and you are not to blame.
You didn't influence him to become TS. His condition is quite unusual and cannot be predicted.
The causes of it are not known, but it is certain that his transsexualism won't go away and will not be cured.
It may have been, and may remain, masked for many years, but eventually, for a TS, it will come out and must be dealt with.
Sooner or later the TS reaches the point where denial and repression are not viable options. Failure to address the overriding need to explore and probably take steps to becoming a woman can lead to mental breakdown

and, in some cases, suicide.

He's your child, you love him and want what is best for him.

He needs to know that you want to understand him, help him and are prepared to discuss your feelings and be honest with one another.

Remember that even though you may be profoundly distressed seeing him dressed as a woman, a TS will do whatever is necessary to effect the change, even though this may mean loss of family, friends, home, job etc. Such is the power of this driving force, the TS will lie, cheat, deceive or do whatever she needs. Some, formerly respectable pillars of the community, have gone into prostitution to enable their changes.

It is not as if medical science has not attempted to intervene. All sorts of methods have been brought into play in an effort to make TSs revert to their original gender role, including horrific aversion therapy, but to no avail.

But this is a problem that does have a solution. The condition of transsexualism can be cured by means of gender reassignment --- more widely known as a sex change.

Whilst this cure may feel like accepting defeat when you should be fighting to help your son develop into the man you always believed he was born to be, please remember that he may well be one of those unusual people whose conception of their gender is at variance with the evidence of their physical sex. Physical sex is denoted by the evidence of genitalia. Gender identity is about how a person feels. The important thing is not how you, or your friends or relatives, feel about his gender: it is how he feels.

Physical sex can be altered. Gender identity, at the current state of medical science, cannot.

Thus the only cure is gender reassignment: matching his gender awareness to the body by changing the body to match the brain's awareness.

The option you face is whether you can be supportive, or whether you must reject your child. Such is the harsh truth.

A gender identity disorder (sometimes referred to as gender dysphoria) is a psycho-sexual complaint. The person who has it is deeply affected by it, but may be perfectly sane, lucid and competent in all other areas. It is not a mental illness in the generally accepted sense of the term.

However, if your son really has this condition, and you are prepared to be supportive throughout, then you will find yourself calling on all your reserves of patience, tact and consideration. You will be accepting a heavy burden, a great emotional weight and, for some time, may feel you are doing this without receiving any appreciation or consideration.

Most TSs diagnose themselves. They are aware that they should be women, should always have been women and desperately want to get things moving in order to become women. Medical practice demands that they must live in role, functioning socially, for a minimum of 12 months prior to being recommended for surgery. During that time, they may well receive feminising hormones which will cause the development of a bust (usually quite small), alter skin tone, slightly soften the facial features, effect the most marginal additional widening of the hips by a slight degree of fat redistribution, soften body hair, have no effect on voice, cause a slight slowing down of beard growth (but the whiskers will remain as coarse as before), reduce muscularity, reduce and possibly eliminate the sex drive. They also tend to produce many of the effects associated with both puberty and menopause: sore nipples, mood changes, weepiness and hot flushes.

They receive hormones on prescription having been interviewed and accepted for the gender reassignment programme by a gender psychiatrist, either privately or at a Gender Identity Clinic.

The referral to the gender specialist is a two stage process. Initially your son sees his GP who recommends a psychiatrist whose task is to assess whether your son may be experiencing gender identity problems and who will, if appropriate, refer him to a psychiatrist specialising in gender identity matters.

Please understand that your son's condition is treatable and you and he will need lots of support and information.

Specialists exist in this field:- it is kinder to all concerned if they are involved sooner rather than later. However, one thing you will want to be certain about in your own mind is whether your son really is TS, or whether there is a chance that he is an over enthusiastic transvestite trying to live out a fantasy; a gay guy who cannot acknowledge his homosexuality or even a man with a desire to have breasts but retain all his male organs in perfect working order.

It is also important that before embarking on the TS route he should fully understand all the implications of his desired course of action. Many parents, and many TSs have found it helpful to have a meeting for an informal discussion at TransLiving. It is an ideal opportunity for parents and TSs alike to ask detailed questions and receive informative answers. It also provides an opportunity for other issues of sexuality to be addressed.

As for the question of your son's sexuality, some TSs had been in gay relationships prior to change, some had been heterosexual (some indeed had entertained liaisons with women, been married and had children) and some had been bisexual. Some had been sexually active prior to change, some were virgins. There's no golden rule.

> 'Mermaids' is an excellent family support group for children and teenagers with gender identity issues.
>
> *(Their helpline number is: 07020 935066 and website on: http://www.mermaids.freeuk.com)*

What would the neighbours say/think? • How could he cope? • Why hadn't I/we realised it before? • Why did he hide it from me/us? • Can I/we get him to change his mind? • How can we cope: what do we tell people? • How on earth will he look? • How long will it take? • How will I feel if he brings a boyfriend home?

Once you have both agreed what is to be done, and assuming he is to pursue gender reassignment, you will need to face the immediate implications of the decision. At some point 'he' will become 'she' for good. That will happen at least a year before the operation. Prior to 'going full-time' he will dress as a woman with increasing frequency. When so dressed, he will expect to be referred to as 'she'. Indeed, there may well be a period when the only time the 'he' will surface is when in public or at work/college/school. Even then, the chosen presentation will probably be deliberately, and increasingly androgynous.

Eventually your new daughter will need to become accustomed to going out in public as a woman. This is something you cannot hide:- for it is an important part of her change. After all, once she is developing secondary female characteristics she will find herself wanting to be noticed as a woman, yet fearful of being read as someone a bit different. Indeed, it is a useful test, for if she cannot face the public, how can she hope to live and socialise successfully.

Although you may feel awkward, it is a great help to her at this most vulnerable stage of her development if you are prepared to be beside her when she goes out, at least initially.

If friends or neighbours ask about her, it is best to be honest about what is happening. However, remember that later she will not want people to know of her past and you will need to be very discreet to help her protect her secret. A good working guide is to tell those who need to know, and then only when you must. It is generally preferable if she does the telling so that she feels in control of this very personal glimpse into her private life.

On the subject of neighbours, perhaps it is worth remembering that few families have no secrets, few families have nothing they would prefer their neighbours did not know. Once they are likely to have noticed a change, it may be best for her (or you if necessary) to be totally up front and admit she has a little problem --- something that has been with her from childhood and that she has tried, in vain, to control.

It is no disgrace to be a TS or to have a TS son. No more than it would be to have a blonde one, or a lad with a stutter, or a redhead. It is just that people often don't understand and jump to all sort of strange, largely unfounded, assumptions.

As far as siblings are concerned, generally Sisters will accept it. Post pubertal brothers often react with acute embarrassment initially.

We know of many cases where youngsters have had their lives rendered miserable through the bullying and cruel teasing of other children who discovered the TS secret of their relative. It may thus be necessary to make teachers aware of the situation so they can watch out for any teasing or bullying.

A parent naturally worries about how the TS child will cope, will look and how long the change will take. Perhaps it is constructive to remember there is little choice: deny the TS the chance to change and she is unlikely to be able to cope at all.

As much as she has recognised her own condition, so too she must be the one who will decide whether she can face the consequences and the ultimate irreversibility of it. A wise parent has little alternative other than to attempt to be supportive and to be ready to stand by and help her if things go badly wrong.

The only other option is to make a clean break if you cannot come to terms with the change. After all, if the chosen gender is totally unacceptable to you, it is better to make a clean break rather than ruin all your lives by living in total misery.

In general, gender reassignment is a successful procedure for TSs, but they still need a great deal of emotional support and reassurance thereafter. Never forget, a TS is always aware that she has a rather different past from other women: she always had a secret that is best kept hidden, and thus will always fear discovery.

For her own protection it is desirable that she should quickly learn how to present herself so she is not too conspicuous. If over 18, she can learn a great deal from joining a self-help TV/TS group, but, in fairness, that has its downside too. She could make contact with people who may persuade her to explore the clubs on the 'gender scene'. She may be flattered by the attention of some of the 'tranny fanciers' (males who are interested in TVs or TSs) and could, possibly, start experimenting sexually.

The thought of this may be horrific for you. However, it is worth remembering that she has a need to understand her own evolving sexuality and, whether you like it or not, she will do whatever she must in order to come to terms with herself. This may mean some sexual adventures that she will learn are not to her taste. It is thus important that she should understand about sexually transmitted disease and the need for safe sex.

There is a seedy side to the 'gender scene'. There are many sexually predatory men out there and a good many 'working girls' of somewhat indeterminate gender. The better groups (and TransEssex is one of the best examples) provide a safe environment in which no unwanted advances will be made and any importunate male will be promptly asked to leave if causing affront to any member or guest.

The question of why he hid his problem from you is simply answered:- despite knowing his feelings for most of his life, he was aware that they 'were not right' and consequently hid them, first perhaps for fear of punishment and/or ridicule, later, as sexual awareness grew, from feelings of guilt and shame.

Because gender awareness is such a fundamental part of human interactions --- you spot a woman at a glance and behave accordingly --- anything that strikes at that awareness provokes great disquiet. We all feel it. So does your TS child. For the TS also knows that what she is planning strikes at the very basis of your attitude to her as a person: for the he you know, love and thought you understood, has become a her, even though initially looking and sounding like a him.

You don't know what other changes will take place. Will you be able to love her as you loved him? You don't know and this uncertainty puts pressure on all the family.

Although your preconceptions have been challenged, you are still dealing with the person you have always loved. It's just that the person is now developing into a female person rather than continuing as a male one. Your child is still your child – she has a rather more complex personality than ever you had imagined.

The fact that you have been so affected by her news should make it no surprise to realise that she must have found it terribly difficult to face up to – and the prospect of telling her nearest and dearest must have been particularly daunting. Small wonder she delayed it, or even as often happens, procrastinated so much that eventually the truth had to come out.

So determined are many TSs to overcome and suppress their transsexualism, that they deliberately choose macho occupations or interests in an attempt to make real men of themselves. It is not uncommon to find TSs who once were paras or motorcycle racers for example.

The question of how long it will take is not simple to address either. From the onset of hormone therapy, it is reasonable to expect breast development liable to be noticed by strangers after some 4 months or so. However, successful transition normally requires beard removal (electrolysis is still the method of choice) and speech therapy too. If your son seeks gender reassignment before having any significant beard growth, then electrolysis may not take many months. Youngsters who have had puberty put on hold by administration of drugs, may need neither electrolysis nor, if the voice had never broken, speech therapy. However, in the majority of cases both will be needed.

Those seeking gender reassignment surgery privately may find it necessary to live in role for a year or so. Normally patients under the NHS must so live for at least two years. During that time they will live as females full time. This is more than just dressing the part. They must truly live it complete with a name change, correction of official records etc. They will face the world in their new role – and face the world's reaction. Until the time of surgery it is not too late to turn back. You need somehow to impart to your child that you understand the need for gender reassignment and that you support it. That you have no doubt that it is right for her – and at the same time, that you will be just as supportive if, for some reason, she ever decides to stop.

It would be truly dreadful if someone suffering gender confusion felt compelled to proceed all the way to gender reassignment just because they told their parents (or anyone else) that is what they were going to do.

Many parents assume the wish to go for reassignment must be a passing fad and that the TS will grow out of it. Some are encouraged to believe that hormone administration is a self-regulating mechanism that sorts the true TS from the simply confused on the assumption that only the true TS will welcome the attendant loss of libido. Experience of dealing with hundreds of TSs convinces us that transsexualism is an issue that must be taken seriously:- it will not go away, and that once taking hormones, most people will continue with them – even those who it is hard to believe ever could be transsexual.

The pre-operative TS knows her former sexuality. She cannot know how she will be afterwards. Many post-op TSs opt for relationships they describe as lesbian (sexual relationships with women). Former gay TSs often seem to continue to have relationship with gay men. Some formerly heterosexual males retain that heterosexual mode and, post operatively, seek relationships as women with men. No individual knows how she will feel.

Indeed, it is not uncommon for TSs to live together. Some will test the water pre-operatively, others will wait.

It is not unusual for TSs who were quite quiet, shy, retiring males to become sexually hyper-active females. Or to put it more bluntly, behave like

promiscuous tarts. It seems that some feel the need to prove something to themselves:- another example of the insecurity to which they seem so prone. If she brings a boyfriend home you have some cause for concern if he does not know her past. Will he react violently upon finding out?
Relationships are a subject that should be discussed with her as part of your support dialogue throughout her transition. She needs to understand the effect her status may have on other people and the risks she could be running. There is probably little more that you can realistically be expected to do.
On the subject of neighbours, perhaps it is worth remembering that few families have no secrets, few families have nothing they would prefer their neighbours did not know. Once they know, it may be best to be totally up front and admit he has a little problem --- something that has been with him from childhood that he has tried, in vain, to control.
It is no disgrace to have a TS son. No more than it would be to have a blonde one, or a lad with a stutter, or a redhead. It is just that people often don't understand and jump to all sort of strange, largely unfounded, assumptions.

With young TSs certain other questions spring to mind:

Might he grow out of it?
Is it better to change before completion of adolescence?
What if his psyche is lagging behind his physical development – who's to say that in five or six years time he wouldn't become a normal healthy male?
Is he simply over impressionable and identifying just too closely with a female figure?
Isn't he just too young to make up his mind over gender and sexuality?
Wouldn't it be best for him to have some experience of life before doing anything irreversible?
Could this just be attention seeking?
Who can I talk to about this?

It is possible that he may grow out of it. Some do. However, if his feelings are so strong that he is absolutely insistent that he should be female, it is probable that he will not.
Those TSs below the age of majority tend to be dealt with by specialist teams. In general they prefer to attempt to delay any form of intervention until past puberty and they can be reasonably sure that the child's eventual sexuality and gender identity have evolved. After all, if there is a chance that the child can become a normal healthy male, it would be very wrong to prevent it happening through premature intervention.
In some cases, if reasonably sure that reassignment is likely, the young TS will be given medication that effectively puts puberty on hold by preventing male pattern beard growth and voice breaking. Youngsters helped in this way often change extremely well and become indistinguishable from other girls their age.
Some youngsters may identify too closely with a female figure, some may be too immature to be trusted to judge their gender and sexuality. But some clearly do know, and for these it is important that there is no undue delay, no undue unwanted physical masculinisation.
We have encountered youngsters convinced they are TS who have fantasised and believed their fantasy.

One such was keen to go on a gender reassignment programme until he found a girlfriend. Suddenly he changed – his manner, even his voice. He is now determinedly male, enjoying an active heterosexual sex life and has put the whole idea of being TS firmly behind him.

He needed a girlfriend to give him the experience he had lacked. He discovered his gender identity and has not looked back. But whilst this works for some, there are some who really are TS and need to change without delay.

In the first instance it will be helpful if you contact TransLiving for a discussion. We may well be able to provide immediate effective help either directly or via our contacts who specialise in the problems of younger TSs and their families.

A meeting of this sort can be particularly useful in enabling both parents and children to confront issues honestly and openly in a way that would be difficult strictly within the family.

It can also present an excellent opportunity for the potential TS to learn far more about the true implications of being transsexual.

What help is there for parents, families and friends of TSs?

In general, precious little. Troubled people tend to have recourse to trusted friends, for Relate, Samaritans and most GPs have little experience in this area.

Groups that cater for TSs tend to have a focus on the TSs and, with the notable exception of TransLiving, are not particularly active in a wider context.

TransLiving provides HelpLine support for parents and siblings. It publishes guides on gender issues and offers the facility for private meetings to consider individual problems in depth. We provide guidance for the TS and will facilitate discussions with parents and the TS together, if appropriate.

Our role is thus broadly that of confidante, mediator, moderator, counsellor and advisor rolled into one.

We can furnish contacts with, or referrals to, other appropriate counsellors and health care professionals when/if the situation merits it.

Transsexualism can easily destroy your relationship with your erstwhile son. Through transition, a lonely, vulnerable and frightening time, the need for your love, care and understanding will never have been greater since his infancy, and the bonding between you and your child could well be greatly strengthened.

Is there anything that will stop this Transsexualism?

The more forcefully you try to set obstacles in the way, the more insistent the TS is likely to become.

Most of them know full well that they risk losing almost everything:- family, friends, career, home, car, earning capacity and social status. Yet they are still prepared to go ahead.

It takes a decision from the TS to stop it all. There are some who, through the misfortune of size, shape, features, voice etc., could never hope to become remotely passable as women, however expensive their wigs or hairstyles, however expert their make-up, however costly and beautiful their clothes, and despite the best efforts of plastic surgeons. A six foot six TS weighing some twenty stone and with size eleven feet is liable to be conspicuous, even if she does grow a bust and develop

softer features.
Some TSs realise that by changing, the quality of life is liable to worsen for them. They may thus come to terms with trying to continue as men, using discreet cross-dressing as a palliative measure.
Those unfortunate TSs feel forced to live a lie.
They too need understanding support.

How about my other children and the reactions of other people?

In our experience, children, particularly prior to the growth of sexual awareness that comes with puberty, are remarkably adaptable and accepting of change. It is often the youngest members of a family that will call parents sharply to order if they forget to use the feminine pronoun or her new female name for their former son.
Children going through puberty will often react with a measure of embarrassment (not surprisingly:- they react that way to all sorts of issues of gender and sexuality when the issues are raised by adults).
It is as difficult to predict how older children will react as it is to predict how other adults will react. It depends on their natures, upbringing, the way they are told, when they are told, how they discovered the truth, how the TS looks and behaves and how they interpret the attitude of the person who broke the news.
As a general guide, women tend to be more accepting than men.
Nevertheless, there are still many who take the view that until you bleed you can't be a woman!
There are still many men whose attitude is that TSs are just guys with their dicks cut off.
Many lesbians see them the same way.

Post-op TSs are of little interest to gay men, whilst heterosexual males may happily get into relationships with them until they get to know. At that point, the TS is at risk of a violent adverse reaction based on the man's anger at having been 'deceived'.
It is not uncommon for men to refer to a TS as an 'it' and treat her with the utmost contempt. Of course, there are TSs who do find wonderful loving partners:- they are not in the majority.

What should I do now?

You are not alone in having these problems. It is important that you keep in touch so that we can review progress together.
It may well be that you could benefit from speaking to other parents and comparing notes:- something we may be able to facilitate by mutual agreement.
There is plenty of support for the TS. Hitherto, there has been precious little for family.
You can help others by contributing articles to TransLife International, a magazine widely read by TSs and those involved with them. You can contact its Agony Aunt column with questions you would like addressed, phone or e mail us at TransLiving.
We respect your confidence in us and rigorously preserve confidentiality.
We hope these notes have been of help and would appreciate feed-back from you, as well as pointers to other factors that you feel should be brought to the fore.
As far as your dealings with your TS child are concerned, please try to reduce the emotional tension in all this by being open and down-to-earth.
He has been assailed by fear and guilt, probably for many years, and it was

both frightening for him, and a great relief, when you got to know.
Try to let him express his feelings and anxieties:- by unloading on you, he is able to ease the stresses on himself.
Of course, accepting his emotional baggage on top of trying to cope with the news that he is a TS is an enormous strain on you – but isn't helping your children through crises – helping to ease their burdens by sharing them – all part of being a caring parent?
Your TS child is driven by a force almost as powerful as the involuntary force that makes children become adult. She must evolve. She will be vulnerable and in need of support.
If you cannot give it, and it is understandable, then please encourage her to seek outside help from a caring and knowledgeable support group.
She will not be alone and she will have a measure of protection from exploitation, someone to call on when in need and a source of valuable, accurate health and welfare information.

A TRANSSEXUAL PARENT

As with so many of the outcomes of transsexualism, it is virtually impossible to predict the effects of a parent's transsexualism on a child.
There are too many variables: the age of the child; the child's gender; the Mother's attitudes; the attitudes of any siblings etc.
As a general guide, if the home is loving, the chances are that a young child will be accepting. However, older children who have become accustomed to a loved father figure may well find the change extremely difficult to cope with, not only on their own account, but also because of peer reactions which are frequently of ridicule.

In the best of possible worlds, a person intending to go through gender reassignment would not have children, or, wait until parental responsibilities are fulfilled.
But this is not such a world and the compulsion to change does not have a habit of coming at the most expedient times.
If the consequence of revealing himself as a transsexual is the breakdown of a marriage, then the sort of problems his children will have are analogous to those involved in divorces for other reasons.
They are just as likely to have conflicts of loyalty, but those conflicts may be further compounded by issues of disapproval from one side and guilt on the other.
Some families manage to hold together: the transitioning taking an interesting turn as the father becomes parent and friend rather than father and husband. Whilst a few can survive the inevitable strains, noone should be under any illusion as to how great those strains can be.
Quite apart from the emotional stresses, the feelings of loss and the sense of betrayal, there are liable to be severe financial constraints. Add too the disapproval of friends and neighbours (likely although not inevitable) and the teasing and possible humiliation faced by children at school and the stresses can easily become too great to handle.
There are a few cases of transsexuals taking on the lone parent role with great success, but it is prudent to assume that in situations where both parents are seeking custody of the children, it remains the general rule that courts look with favour on the mother.

Of course, there is no reason on earth why a TS single parent should be any better or worse than any other single parent:- some will be good parents, some not so good. However, there is the added complication that the children will almost certainly have to take on some of the baggage associated with transsexualism. They are the ones who will be aware of snide comments from other children, of cutting remarks overheard. They will be conscious that their parent is not quite the same as the other Mums. They may be inordinately proud of her; rally to her defence at every opportunity and love her dearly. But they still have to take on some of the TS linked baggage and that is a great burden for them to have to bear.

AN INFORMAL GUIDE TO THE OP.

Gender Reassignment Surgery (GRS), commonly known as 'the Op.' amongst transsexuals, and as 'the sex change' to the public at large, is a procedure to remove evidence of male genitalia and remodel them as a cosmetically accurate representation of natural female genitalia with or without useful depth.

Although there are minor procedural differences between surgeons, the fundamentals are as follows.

The transsexual (TS) has some choices:

1   A purely cosmetic procedure whereby the external appearance of the labia is convincing, but the neo vagina has insufficient depth to permit penetrative sex.

2   Creation of genitalia incorporating labia minor and major and a neo-vagina of sufficient depth to permit penetrative sex.

3   As in #2 above, with the addition of a sensitive apparent clitoris.

The procedures involve the reuse of the penile tissue, the cutting away of the flesh of the penis (apart from a section of the glans and the nerves that serve it in #3) and the cutting back of the urethra and its resiting in a position analogous to that of the natural female. Testes are excised, but the scrotal tissue (skin covering) and penile tissue sewn in such a way as to create the labia and neo vagina which is then invaginated into a perianal cavity created for the purpose (an opening cut some 2" or so forward of the anus. The vaginal opening is thus sited in virtually the same position as in a natural female. In choice #3, the neo-clitoris is positioned precisely where the natural female clitoris would be found.

Some candidates for surgery have such small genitals that the surgeons cannot find sufficient tissue to model a vagina with useful depth. A more complex operation can then be carried out. It involves cutting a section of the lower intestine and adding that to the penile and scrotal tissue to form the neo-vagina.

#1 is cheaper than the other procedures, but will not stand the test of normal sexual intercourse. It may be recommended for older candidates for surgery who feel they do not want vaginal intercourse, or those people whose male organs could not furnish sufficient skin to create a functional vagina and for whom a more complex operation would not be advisable.

#2 seems to offer few advantages for it is the same as #3 except that no clitoris is created.

#3, the most popular procedure, is so convincing that many TSs experience satisfying intercourse, complete with orgasm, without their partners being aware of the fact that they were not born female.

The operation is irreversible. For this reason, in order to protect the interests of the TS, and legally safeguard the surgeon and psychiatrist, no procedure will be entertained without the surgeon being convinced that the TS understands what will be done and how it cannot be reversed, and without his having the recommendation and referral for surgery from the psychiatrist supervising the gender reassignment programme supported by a second opinion by an independent psychiatrist.

Few TSs will succeed in foreshortening the period of the 'real life test' – that time during which the pre-op TS is expected to live as, work as and socialise as a woman. Indeed, this is a valuable trial run for living as a woman. At least the TS has a chance to opt out if she should so wish. She will be given that same chance right up to the last minute. She will be asked whether she wishes to go ahead with the surgery before being given her anaesthetic.

Those having private treatment may get through this in a year or so. Those going via the NHS must expect a minimum of two years.

Six weeks or so prior to surgery the TS must come off her hormone treatment. This is a precautionary measure designed to minimise the risk of thrombosis following surgery. (Thai & Belgian surgeons may require 2 weeks, but 6 weeks seems to be a wise measure.) Some three to four weeks before admission the TS will attend for blood tests and be tested for HIV infection.

At this stage, the hospital or clinic will generally provide the services of a counsellor (possibly a specially trained nurse) who will explain what is involved and the implications of and need for the HIV test.

Typically, the op. requires a hospital stay of some 8 to 10 days. Normally the hospital likes the patient to have time to settle in and relax. They introduce the members of the duty team and ask whether she has any questions. They will explain the procedure and what to expect.

Once settled in, having not eaten since the previous day, the transsexual's bowels are evacuated. This may involve use of suppositories and may well include colonic irrigation, a procedure involving a funnel, warm soapy water, a length of hose and several frantic dashes to the loo with legs clamped tightly together!

A rather unglamorous start to proceedings, but it is important that faecal matter is kept well out of the way of the site of surgery.

The next day she will have a pre-med and go to surgery. Before losing consciousness, she will once again be asked whether she has any doubts about going ahead and it will be impressed upon her that it is still not too late to call a halt to proceedings if she feels any uncertainty.

She awakes to the knowledge that she is continuing on a liquid diet for five days, has a nappy like dressing between her legs and that she has a collection of tubes coming into and out of different areas. She has to wear heavy white surgical stockings during her hospital stay – a further precaution against deep vein thrombosis. After twenty-four hours of feeling quite sleepy (the expected reaction to anaesthesia) she will drowse and browse her way through the time until the fifth day when her packing will be removed. The passage of time will be marked by nurses coming in to check the wound, change drips, dress the wound and apply antiseptic creams to the stitches (biodegradable type), check the urine bag (she was catheterised at the time of the op and will remain like that for some eight days), hand out any painkillers required (many TSs do not need any at all) and refresh the supply of water or hot (milk free) drinks:- black tea or Bovril being typical. Meals are typically more Bovril and clear jelly.

The neo-vagina gradually heals up over the five post-op days, but internally is well packed with wadding to absorb blood and keep the vagina stretched and open.

Unless the TS has completed her course of electrolysis to get rid of her beard, there is every chance that by the time she has recovered enough to realise it, she will have a healthy looking stubble which will have grown faster than normal for her on account of her having come off the hormones for so long. She thus needs to be sure she has packed shaving materials and that they are in easy reach while she is still bed-bound. Naturally she will need to ask for a bowl of hot water and to avoid embarrassment, should request posting of a 'do not disturb' notice while she gets rid of the offending growth.

On that fifth day the TS can have her first meal of solids. She will also have the novel experience of lying on her back with legs raised in a frog position so her surgeon can reach into her vagina and remove the packing.

Although this sounds fairly unpleasant, the TS will normally be relaxed --- one describes how she was given gas and couldn't stop giggling: in fact she was high as a kite and quite happy to let the surgeon grope for as long as he wanted!

Once the packing is out, the TS can get up and go for a bath. She will be escorted by a couple of nurses in case she is wobbly. The bath is especially welcome and very necessary, for a tremendous amount of clotted blood and mess floats from the vagina. This excursion to the bathroom also introduced the TS to the dubious pleasure of moving around with a permanently attached urine bag.

The next interesting item will be learning about dilation:- the procedure that will be a twice daily ritual for quite some time. It involves the insertion of a well lubricated dilator, an acrylic rod shaped rather like a candle, which is helps keep the vagina stretched to its full length. A nurse will come and explain what to do. Some hospitals encourage TSs to dilate in the bath --- the water constituting a useful additional lubricant.

Typically, the dilator is well larded with a toffee-like antiseptic (Betadine) and KY jelly. Most TSs start by using a smaller diameter dilator for a few minutes, remove it and then try the slightly larger one. After a few days they will be dilating for quarter of an hour with each dilator, twice per day for a month to six weeks (at which point the betadine will be phased out), gradually working towards using just the larger dilator for half hour periods. By the time six months have passed, the TS should be dilating once per week, unless she is having regular intercourse, in which case dilation is not necessary. We normally recommend TSs to use Senselle (available from most chemists) once they stop using Betadine on their dilator/s. It is an excellent lubricant that closely resembles natural body secretions and is far less messy than KY.

Once having been able to get out of bed for her bath, the TS is free to wander round at will. She will tire easily and probably be surprised at how slight her energy reserves seem.

It is important that the TS should understand that wiping clean following defecation involves a wipe from front to back in order to ensure no faecal matter is wiped over the wound, vagina, urethra, clitoris or labia.

On the eighth day she will have her catheter removed:- a painless procedure. If she can urinate freely, it will stay out. If she cannot pass water successfully, she will be re-catheterised for a further day or so. Most TSs find that passing water involves a bit of a wait and then a surprising 'helicopter' spray in which the urine rushes out in a rotary action like a helicopter rotor blade, going everywhere but straight down. However, this phase quickly passes and the TS should soon pee like the best of women.

The next thing is for her to go home (9th or 10th day). The very last bit of attention will be the removal of any stitch residues by a nurse. She will need to use sanitary towels and panty liners for the first week or so after leaving hospital, for she will have some bloody exudate. Thereafter she should be clean as a whistle. The hospital will be anxious to establish that she is going to have someone to drive her home and to be around to keep half an eye on her. They will send her home with her dilators.

Post operatively few have complications and they should be sent away with some clear instructions about personal hygiene, after-care and necessary cautions.

For two to three weeks post operatively, the TS will probably apply topical antiseptic to the stitch line. Provided it has healed well, it is desirable to discontinue the antiseptic treatment to allow the natural flora to return.

There is considerable swelling around the genitals post operatively, and it takes quite some time to disappear. The area where the urethra is sited initially looks to have a gaping aperture, but this closes over the ensuing months. Indeed, the swelling may take some three months to clear. Although there is so much swelling, it does not seem to cause pain or significant discomfort. Many TSs find sitting in one position for a long time tiresome in the first few weeks after surgery.

The TS should keep her vagina fresh by periodic (monthly) vaginal douche using betadine and a douche bottle, or betadine via an applicator. She should flush it daily using a douche bottle (a douche bottle is often supplied by the hospital, but if not, comes as part of a betadine vaginal douche kit from the chemist). Some TSs find it satisfactory to use a soft shower hose to flush out the vagina:- but they should be careful to avoid high pressures and be careful over water temperatures.

Because the neo-vagina is lined with skin rather than mucosa, it is not self lubricating and the TS will need to use a lubricant when making love, using a dilator or dildo.

She should not contemplate intercourse for at least four months post operatively:- six may be prudent. She should have a medical certificate covering at least four weeks off work, more if heavy work is involved. She should regard her operation as somewhat akin to a hernia op in terms of taking care not to lift heavy objects and, in the first few weeks she should be particularly careful.

One month after her op she will get her '1000-mile check' when her surgeon will look at his handiwork. Having pronounced himself satisfied, the TS is on her own. She's had her op. She has become the woman she wanted to be. She is a statistical success and must get on with her life.

After some time she may be alarmed by a smelly fibrous bundle loose in her vagina. It is a hair ball formed from pubic hairs that grew inside, rotted and became matted together. Some TSs get this: many do not.

The operation is a profound landmark for the TS. Her socialisation as a woman will continue, for she still has much to learn. However, the handicap of male organs has been rectified. She cannot conceive, she cannot have periods, but she has gained the body form she knows to be right for her.

Two to four weeks after she leaves hospital, she will be permitted to go back onto her hormones. She will continue hormone therapy through life. Initially it had been for its feminising effects. At this stage it is merely a maintenance dose which has the advantage of preventing the onset of osteoporosis. There is no need to maintain the same levels of hormone ingestion as pre-operatively. In fact, it is to be avoided and the GP should be requested to reduce the prescribed dose accordingly.

He may well wish to consult with the psychiatrist who had been responsible for helping the TS through the gender reassignment programme.

Most TSs leave hospital on a high. They have achieved what they wanted. They feel complete and they feel physically and mentally right. They are convinced, delighted and vulnerable. After all, the world outside may not see them as complete women. Many find, after the initial period of euphoria, that post-operative isolation is a marked anti-climax following all the pre operative excitement – visits to the psychiatrist, the GP, the hospital etc. It is not uncommon for them to become depressed.

In truth, they still need support and guidance. They still need understanding friends and knowledgeable contacts. They are still vulnerable people who frequently need the emotional crutch of someone who will listen to their problems, share their joys and to whom they can look for guidance. TransLiving is positioned to offer that sort of support, for it can draw upon the experience of having helped countless transsexuals from their earliest recognition of their condition right through to surgery and beyond.

Please note: the above information provides a general guide. Some hospitals do not provide dilators (sometimes called 'stints'), merely recommending use of a dildo. Different surgeons carry out the procedure in different ways:- TSs should ask their surgeons how they perform the op. --- whether in one stage as described, or as a two-step procedure involving a preliminary orchidectomy (removal of testes) and the length of post operative stay in hospital, or is transfer to a nursing home required?

Post-op transsexuals should follow the

specific after care instructions given to them by the hospital/clinic where they had been treated.

WHERE TO GO FOR THE OP

One of the advantages of treatment in the UK is that it is on home ground. You know the language, you understand the healthcare system.
Whilst there may be financial arguments in favour of having surgery abroad, can you be sure that the hygeine standards are adequate?
Are you thinking of having surgery in a Third World country?
Can you be sure that the Surgeon is properly qualified?
How confident would you be of the level of care to screen blood supplied for a possible transfusion?
What recourse do you have if there are complications after the operation?
If you are dissatisfied with any aspects of your operation and care, to whom do you complain?
Is there post-op after care available?
If you are in difficulties, will there be English speaking staff who can understand you? (Remember there is a great deal of difference between understanding enough English to know if a patient is requesting a drink and that required to understand a description of a particular type of discomfort.
As with many purchases in life, it can be a good idea to talk to someone who has purchased already. Ask them about the experience, find out if they are satisfied with the outcome. It may be far more difficult to find someone who has been to a remote country for surgery.
TransLiving does not recommend particular surgeons. After all, different surgeons use different techniques and they result in different outcomes. Each surgeon is likely to refine and modify his technique over time: it is the responsibility of each TS undertaking this elective procedure to satisfy herself that the surgeon's technique produces the outcome she wants and that she has full confidence in the surgeon and clinic or hospital that she will attend for surgery and in the after-care arrangements.

PRIVATE OR NHS --- WHICH IS BETTER?

If you can afford private treatment and as a result are able to secure surgery after a year of the real life test (rather than two as is standard for NHS cases) then you may well feel the significant expense to be worthwhile.
If you have private treatment you may be able to combine GRS with a boob job, if you really feel that is what you need.
Private treatment is expensive and could take place in an NHS facility. Above all, you are paying for the quicker lead time before surgery and avoiding any delays through the effective quota system by which only limited funds are released for this type of surgery, priority being given to other procedures that are considered more important and that are certainly less contentious.
If you do not have the private means, then the NHS system will be your choice.
It is worth noting that patients who sit back and wait until 'Buggins turn' are likely to sit back and wait forever. The system does not go out of its way to push you forward. After all, if you are content to identify yourself as a transsexual, see a psychiatrist every three to six months and wait for him to tell you that you are ready for surgery,

then you will be likely to have a very long wait indeed.

The flip side of this is that many practitioners in the NHS feel that those in private practice are pushing TSs along, and as a result may be steering them towards an irreversible procedure and an uncertain future for which they are not fully prepared.

FREQUENTLY ASKED QUESTIONS.
Dr Russell Reid provides the answers

We gather that some TSs are being prescribed oestrogel:- we would like to have information about it: mode of action, effects, side effects, contra indications etc. One question asked of us has been whether its application has any systemic effect and, if so, could it therefore amount to increasing the dose of feminising hormone (Premarin, Ovran or ethinyloestradiol).
Oestrogel
This is an oestrogen, oestradiol 0.06% gel in a pressurised dispenser, 80 gms (64-dose unit, when used twice-daily lasts 32 days). Its normal use is hormone replacement therapy in post menopausal women to relieve vaso-motor symptoms, meaning hot flushes and night sweats as well as atrophic vaginitis and atrophic urethritis, meaning dry vagina and urethra, which is a common complaint of older women. In Transsexuals the gel is rubbed into arms, legs, face and neck, and oestrogen enters the system through the skin, supplementing existing oestrogen from oral preparations or transdermal skin patches. Many Transsexuals report improved skin texture and some even claim reduced hairiness. Transdermal oestrogen including oestrogel is said to have a very low risk of causing phlebitis, deep vein thromboses or pulmonary emboli, compared with oral oestrogens, and so it seems unlikely that oestrogel increases these risks. Oestrogel should be used with caution in persons with heart, liver or kidney disease, or persons with a past history or family history of thrombo-phlebitis, deep vein thrombosis or pulmonary emboli.

We would like to know about the hair restorative tablets that are designed to overcome the problem of male pattern baldness?
Finasteride or Proscar
2.5 to 5mgs daily is said to be a useful scalp hair-restorer. Finasteride is used in the treatment of benign prostatic hypertrophy and is a selective 5-alpha reductase inhibitor that blocks the conversion of Testosterone to Di-hydro-testosterone (DHT). DHT is the form of Testosterone responsible for male pattern baldness, and ironically, hirsutism or genetically determined body hair occurring in males after puberty. Finasteride has little or no effect on established hirsutism, nor on beard growth, and in this regard is not as effective as Androcur (Cyproterone acetate). Most Transsexuals have found Finasteride to be a disappointing scalp hair-restorer.

A TS Member has been asking about the desired frequency of blood chemistry tests whilst on the relatively high level of hormones during the pre-op phase. She also wanted to know what tests should be sought – and why. It would be useful if we could suggest an ideal timetable for her, and others like her, to put to their GPs. Similarly, it would help us justify the need for the various tests if we are in a position to point out their significance.

Frequency of blood chemistry tests pre-operatively

According to the Harry Benjamin guidelines,

"For those receiving oestrogens, the minimum laboratory assessment should consist of a pre-treatment Free Testosterone level, Fasting Glucose, Liver Function Tests, and Complete Blood Count with reassessment at 6 and 12 months and annually thereafter. A pre-treatment prolactin level should be obtained and repeated at 1, 2 and 3 years.

If hyper-prolactinaemia does not occur during this time, no further measurements are necessary.

For those receiving Androgens, the minimum laboratory assessment should consist of pre-treatment Liver Function Tests and Complete Blood Count with reassessment at 6 months, 12 months, and yearly thereafter. Yearly palpation of the liver should be considered.

Patients should be screened for Glucose intolerance and Gall Bladder disease.

In addition to these investigations, persons taking oestrogens or androgens should have annual checks for Lipid Levels including cholesterol and Tri-glycerides.

Oestrogen doses in post-orchidectomy patients can be reduced by a third and still maintain feminisation. Similarly *[for F>M TSs]* reductions in Testosterone doses after 3-5 years or following oophorectomy should be considered, taking into account the risks of osteoporosis. Long term maintenance treatment is usually required in both sexes".

Medical side effects

Side effects in biological males treated with oestrogens may include increased propensity to blood clotting (venus thrombosis with a risk of fatal pulmonary embolism), development of benign pituitary prolactinomas, infertility, weight gain, emotional lability, and liver disease.

Side effects in biological females treated with Testosterone may include infertility, acne, emotional lability (including the potential for major depression), increases in sexual desire, shift of lipid profiles to male patterns (which increase the risk of cardiovascular disease) and the potential to develop benign and malignant liver tumours and hepatic dysfunction.

Patients with medical problems or otherwise at risk for cardiovascular disease may be more likely to experience serious or fatal consequences of cross-sex hormone treatments. For example, cigarette smoking, obesity, advanced age, heart disease, hypertension, clotting abnormalities, malignancy, and some endocrine abnormalities are relative contra-indications for the use of hormonal treatment. Therefore, some patients may not be able to tolerate cross-sex hormones. However risk-benefit ratios should be considered collaboratively between the patient and prescribing Physician.

Another frequent request concerns long-term after care. Are there any specific checks that post op TSs should take, apart from feeling breasts for lumps, observing scrupulous personal hygiene, dilating and continuing on hormones to offset the problem of osteoporosis. Is there a medical consensus view on the levels of hormone they should be maintained on?

Long term after care
Long term after care should include regular health checks from your GP to include weight and blood pressure every six months, blood tests including liver function and lipid levels every year, and possibly a hormone screen and bone density estimation to exclude osteoporosis every 5-10 years. (Hormone screens may be misleading and a cause of confusion to both the GP and patient. For example, serum oestradiol levels are always very low for patients taking Ethinyloestradiol. This is because the assay for "oestradiol" does not measure "Ethinyloestradiol". As far as I know, there is no standard test for measuring serum Ethinyloestradiol. As well, patients on oestrogens invariably have raised prolactin levels often 2 or 3 times normal, which is predictable and expected. (It is only when the prolactin levels reach 4 or 5 times normal male values that further investigations are required).

Post-operative hormone preparations and doses
Post-operative hormone preparations and doses tend to vary from patient to patient. Most post-operative Transsexuals are maintained on half or 2/3rds of their pre-operative oestrogen dosage. Some like the addition of progesterone including Provera 5mgs once or twice daily, which may improve libido, skin sensitivity and subjective well being. (For other patients however, Provera causes headaches, weight gain, and hirsutism).

There is no standard medical consensus on appropriate postoperative hormone maintenance. The best advice is to find a doctor who is interested and knowledgeable about hormone use in Transsexuals and who is flexible in providing a variety of preparations until the correct combination is found. There are very few Endocrinologists in the UK, either in the NHS or private practice, who are experienced and knowledgeable in the use and monitoring of hormones in Transsexual patients.

WHEN IS IT BEST TO HAVE THE OP?
The right time is when you have experienced the real life test, a protracted period of time of living in role that permits you to reflect on whether this is right for you for life and gives your psychiatrist the chance to see that you are well adjusted in your new role and that the proposed surgery seems appropriate for you.

It is a fact that those who can transition early in life (before the voice breaks, before the beard grows and the body develops its heavy male musculature) certainly are liable to find that they experience far fewer problems in being accepted as female without question. They also tend to find the effects of hormone therapy are a little more marked so that they may well attain bust development typical of other female members of their family. However, the medical profession is extremely wary of recommending young people for treatment, opting instead to permit them to reach majority when they can decide for themselves.

In some cases a decision will be made to put adolescent development on hold by giving medical treatment to prevent the development of secondary sexual characteristics that are considered likely to be unhelpful in the long term.

WHAT ABOUT OTHER FEMINISING SURGERY?

The plastic surgeon can change your appearance, modify your body, but cannot reshape your mind.

It is possible for him to make a man look like a woman: but not possible for him to make a man into a woman.

If you feel that the only way you can become female is with GRS plus some combination of breast enhancement; liposuction; reshaping of the chin, nose and forehead; nose job; face lift; shaving of the Adam's apple; voice surgery; rib removal or jaw line revision, then reflect carefully whether you are expecting the change to be done to you, rather than being an expression of what is already within you.

Remember too that few women receive masses of plastic surgery: they do not expect to look perfect, just as naturally nice as they can. If the only way you can feel acceptable as a woman is by multiple surgical procedures, then you have a problem and it may not be that you are a TS.

However, it is true that for some TSs there can be good reasons for considering some additional surgery. A nose job can make a profound difference to the way a face is perceived, while a tracheal shave can eliminate the problem caused by a prominent Adam's apple.

In order to qualify for GRS you need to live as a woman for at least a year. If you treat that 'real life test' as a sensible trial run, you will readily discover that your 'passing' is much more a matter of your attitude, your confidence and your perception of yourself as a woman than simply of appearance.

It is interesting to note that there are many TVs who look very good when dressed but who are read as males as soon as they step outside the door. Similarly, a good many TSs with far less care over presentation, go blithely through life being accepted as female. Why? Part of the answer is that they know they are women, have the confidence to step out undaunted and can mix comfortably with other women anywhere.

If you sidestep this vital test and manage to convince your gender psychiatrist that you are carrying it out, then the only person that matters is being cheated – and that's you.

A man who wears a dress and make-up does not become a woman, even if he could conceivably pass as one. Similarly, a man who has extensive surgery to gain an appearance that enables him to pass as a woman, merely appears to be a woman: the surgery does not help him become one. On the other hand, a TS may well gain in confidence if surgery facilitates her passing. Thus if she has features that adversely affect her quality of life, there is a case for using surgery as a remedy. If the goal is simply to acquire a figure that accords to male fantasy, then question your motives.

It is undoubtedly true that skilled plastic surgeons can eliminate many typically male characteristics, but at a cost. Perhaps the wisest course is to try to settle into your new life. If it then emerges that remedial surgery will overcome problems you are experiencing on account of physical characteristics you cannot mask or hide, then consider the option of corrective surgery.

I THINK I AM A TS – BUT HOW DO I KNOW

If you need someone else to tell you, then start having severe doubts.

You may be a TS who is not yet ready to take the plunge: a person still battling gender dysphoria but able to maintain a male life style and make do with cross-dressing.

You may be intersexed and feel pressure to conform to one of the binary gender roles.

You may be a TV who thinks that it is wrong for a man to want to wear dresses and that therefore you must really be a woman in a man's body.

You may be a man who is attracted submissively to other men, but for whom the idea of a gay relationship is culturally unacceptable. The only acceptable construct for you may thus seem to be that you are really a woman with a man's body. In truth, the more probable explanation would be that you are a gay male who has not been able to come to terms with his sexuality. In such a case, taking the TS route would be to take the rather extreme measure of castration.

Perhaps the best guide is that if you can cope as you are – then cope. If you cannot, then you should seriously reflect on all the possible reasons why you feel as you do

If you have doubts, then don't go taking serious steps down the TS route, for it can be an alluring path to disaster.

GOING DOWN THE TS ROAD – WHY IT'S OFTEN AN ALLURING PATH TO DISASTER

It is a wonderful thing that people are able to express their diverse sexualities more openly these days.

It has been greatly rewarding to see the comfort many thousands of trannies have derived from being part of a group, from knowing they are not the only ones and that they can dress openly, albeit in safe surroundings.

The down side to all this is that far too many GUYS get carried away by what should be harmless fantasies and decide it would be wonderful to grow their own breasts and to be women. But it is not the breast that makes a real woman a woman. It certainly helps boost her confidence in her femininity, but she is no less a woman after a mastectomy than before.

Transpeople need to understand that gender reassignment is not about wearing pretty clothes and swanning around being admired.

It involves the taking of potent, body altering drugs. Without proper medical supervision, they can be lethal.

Black market drugs should be avoided at all costs. By black market we include all hormone preparations not dispensed by prescription given under proper, qualified medical supervision. The wife's pill, a load of tablets from a venal TS, a purchase via the Internet or from some retail source – they all involve unacceptable levels of risk.

Most of us are appalled at the cynical disregard of life shown by drug peddlers. How many more cases like that of Leah Betts are going to occur because of the greed of a few at the expense of the many youngsters seeking pleasure. Is there so much difference between them and those who seek pleasure through drug induced feminisation? And much difference between the different merchants of drugs?

Gender reassignment involves a traumatic change of lifestyle, of ways of thinking, of attitudes and of relationships.

Indeed, far too many TSs end up isolated, lonely, poor and friendless. After all, many had trouble living their lives as men, the role they had been brought up into and were most familiar with. Is it reasonable to assume they would necessarily do better as women? They pass through a transitional phase, being neither one thing nor the other: an embarrassing phase for them and all those in contact with them.

Vulnerable and facing an uncertain future, they may well attempt to hold onto their former partners:- yet they are changing and that was never part of the original bargain.

They have undertaken a journey into unknown territory. What will be their eventual sexuality? They don't know. Will they pass satisfactorily? They don't know.

Will they be able to secure and sustain employment?

They don't know.

What will be the effects of all the drugs they must take (for life)? Will they put on lots of weight? Or lose their hair? Or have seriously elevated blood pressure?

They don't know.

And have they sought to change to escape in pursuit of just a dream?

Then there are the costs. In order to secure rapid progress, it is usually necessary to secure private treatment. Assume a budget of £800 - £1000 or so for the Psychiatrists; £150 upwards for drugs (assuming they are prescribed on the NHS); a substantial figure for beard removal (budget for £8000 and hope for less); gender reassignment surgery (assume £10500) and add a contingency sum of £4000 for each additional surgical requirement from the following list: breast augmentation, vocal chord surgery and Adam's apple flattening, nose job, face lift.

Compared to the cost of a new car, it's not bad. But the figures can look prohibitive to someone profoundly affected by gender dysphoria and not functioning too well as a result, particularly when facing probable loss of work, income and possibly home as well.

The lower cost option is to wait for NHS treatment. Some have to wait for years.

Indeed, some dither – passing into treatment for a while, living as women for a spell, finding it tough and reverting, then, a while later doing the same thing again.

Now there's nothing wrong with uncertainty --- but surely it is folly to keep making the same mistakes, to keep testing the water and stepping back, to keep a life in a state of flux for years.

The removal of the male beard, and the elimination of the need to shave, is a far bigger problem than most TVs realise. Sure you can mask a beard with Dermablend for an evening out. But it looks decidedly odd to be heavily made up at 7.30 am when the postman calls, or at 9am when you start work --- particularly on a hot summer's day. To get rid of the beard it is necessary to let it grow before each treatment so the operator can see and feel what she is treating – and that's a huge problem for a TS, because who wants to have to go out as a bearded lady?

Of course, the TS needs to build a new wardrobe – most tranny wardrobes are entirely unsuitable for normal life and, generally a priority item, there's the need to develop a new voice.

Here again there is uncertainty. Speech therapy (widely available on the NHS) is necessary, but not all TSs can change their voices satisfactorily. For all practical purposes, the voice cannot settle until the TS is living full time in her new rôle. There is no guarantee that even then it will be good enough to pass muster all day, every day, in the varied situations in which a woman will typically find herself.

The TS must also learn to accept graciously the things that women have been brought up to accept:- the patronising unfairness of the workplace, the bland assumption that she will be happy to wash his dirty socks, underpants etc., and clean the loo after he has carelessly splashed it and its surroundings.

And then there's the secrecy. The TS doesn't want her past revealed, for she knows from (usually bitter) experience that people undergo a remarkable change of attitude when they know. Many say they won't care because they are living the life they have always wanted. Bullshit!

Who wants to be pointed out as something different throughout life. Every TS wants to be accepted in her new life without demur, without question, without an awareness that there's always somebody pointing the finger and spilling the beans.

But no matter how well the past is hidden, there's always someone, somewhere. Always the fear of exposure, the fear that someone feels it their duty to tell a friend.

If she has a relationship with a man, he may happily screw her if he does not know, but on finding out go completely wild and attack her viciously. If she lets him know her secret in advance, he may well heap insults on her, reject her outright and shout her secret to the four winds.

Many people find the very idea of a transsexual repugnant and seem to think any TS is a freak, pervert and probably a prostitute for good measure. She is likely to be ostracised socially and some are thus marginalised so much that they need to resort to prostitution in order to survive.

The simple truth is that the transsexual road is a dangerous and uncertain one. Noone should even attempt to tackle it unless the risks and the uncertainties are clearly understood.

A transsexual is not a more advanced TV: the two have entirely different motivations. A TV who looks good and can pass on occasional trips out is not ready qualified to 'go full time' – whatever that means.

Imagine how nonplussed he is liable to be if he were to get involved in conversations about menstruation, the change of life, childbirth, hysterectomies, relationships with guys, child rearing, breast feeding, ovarian and breast cancers as a matter of routine, quite apart from occasional chats about the relative sizes of different dicks and the disappointing performance of various individuals.

Sure, men can tell dirty jokes, but women are quite happy to get into the most intimate detail of matters both medical and sexual.

If you can cope with remaining a tranny, then you are well advised to do so.

After all, you can be discreet about it so that it does not affect you at work and does not threaten your income earning potential.

Now many prospective TSs argue that their capabilities are the same before and after, so they should not suffer financially.

True, they should not. But in this real world, it is almost certain that they will!

A TV can be a guy amongst the lads in the pub or at a football match, he can pursue all his old interests and still successfully keep a home and family whilst having his transvestism too.

He can enjoy the feel of different fabrics, the sexual thrill of particular garments, enjoy the gentle pleasures of pampering himself and attempting to portray his dream woman.

But when it's all over, he can strip, shower, stick his boobs in the drawer, his wig on its block and carry on as normal in the rôle he has grown into. His transvestism is quite simply an expression of his male sex drive and in the majority of cases no indication whatsoever of incipient transsexualism. Indeed, this point is evidenced by the frequently expressed wish of many TVs that their partner should have sex with them when they are cross dressed. Many of those would be bitterly disappointed to discover that one of the frequently experienced effects of female hormones is a lowering of the libido, so much so that the stiff prick becomes merely a fond memory.

And one other thing to bear in mind. A TV can continue with his sexual relationships without a problem.

Go have gender reassignment and you won't know how your sexuality will end up.

We've seen some set up home with lesbians: some cohabit with fellow TSs: some continue to have relationships with gay males in precisely the same way as before; some have relationships with straight males and some seem to be completely asexual.

It is not uncommon for them to go completely off the rails and start putting themselves around. It seems such a shame for somebody to go through the whole programme in order to end up as the local bike.

The transsexual route is one strewn with pitfalls, yet it seems to have an almost fatal allure.

Anyone who needs to have his life and body altered so drastically must have had a dreadful problem. Gender reassignment may well alleviate some of the problems, but that person is still likely to remain very vulnerable and never able to shake off the ghost of her past.

TRANSSEXUAL ATHLETE ADVISES CYCLIST TO QUIT
– FORMER TENNIS STAR REGRETS FIGHTING FOR RIGHT TO PLAY (CANADA)

The Canadian cyclist in a fight to race against women even though she was born a man should give up her campaign, the sporting world's most famous transgendered athlete said yesterday.

Michelle Dumaresq is to race for Canada in the women's downhill event at the world championships of mountain biking today in Kaprun, Austria. But Renée Richards, the one-time tennis great who had a surgical sex change in 1975, then fought with the sport's governing bodies for the opportunity to play as a woman, warned Ms. Dumaresq to give up her fight.

"Cease and desist, I would tell her," said Dr. Richards, now 68 and a paediatric ophthalmologist practising in New York. "It's very sad for her, but that ultimate acceptance she will not get."

On this, the 25th anniversary of her legendary appearance in the

Women's U.S. Open, Dr. Richards said Ms. Dumaresq's is a no-win situation: She can lose races such as today's and not be happy with her performance. Or, she can win, thereby lending credence to arguments that her male past gives Ms. Dumaresq an unfair edge.

"It's an absolute Catch-22," Dr. Richards said. The remarks were some of the first by Dr. Richards, née Richard Raskind, to a reporter since 1981. That was when she left the women's professional tennis circuit following a bitter, high-profile legal fight with the sport's powers-that-be for the right to play tennis against other women.

She won the legal battle and went on to play against an elite group that included Billy Jean King, Chris Evert and Martina Navratilova, whom she later coached to Wimbledon victory. But at the end of it, she regretted ever putting herself through it, Dr. Richards said in an interview.

Given the chance, she said she would reverse her decision in 1976 to fight for the opportunity to play professional tennis.

"I would've never done it. I never would have competed in the professional realm and I never would have let myself be uncovered like that," she said.

She also called Ms. Dumaresq's experiences in vying for a spot this year on Canada's national mountain biking team proof that not much has changed for transgendered athletes since Dr. Richards' days playing professional tennis.

Ms. Dumaresq's struggle began last year when the Canadian Cycling Association granted her request for a racing licence, then quickly decided to suspend it following complaints from other riders. The group has since reinstated her licence, a decision backed by its parent, the International Cycling Union.

But this year, Ms. Dumaresq is facing opposition from her fellow riders. A pair of her teammates on Canada's national squad was behind a petition calling for Ms. Dumaresq's removal from women's competition and the creation of a category, called "transgendered," for her to compete in.

In her 1983 autobiography, Second Serve: The Renée Richards Story, Dr. Richards described similar encounters. She was barred from playing in most of the leading tennis tournaments because they were all sanctioned by the Women's Tennis Association and the United States Tennis Association, both of which refused to let Dr. Richards play unless she submitted to a chromosome test.

The book describes how, after winning a pair of exhibition matches against Bobby Riggs at the Ontario Speedway in Brockville, Ont., she decided to take the two organizations to court.

In 1977, she won the case and a shot at the major tournaments. Though in her early 40s, she even won some of them and had other near misses — most notably, the finals of the 1978 Seattle edition of the Virginia Slims, which she barely lost to Ms. Evert — before finally retiring from the professional circuit in 1981.

Someone like Ms. Dumaresq is welcome to try again to pave the way for transgendered athletes, Dr. Richards said, "but they're going to end up not being happy in their pursuit because even if they're successful, they fail."

*[Source: National Post (Canada).
Author: Jon Bricker
Received via: Transgender News
(http://groups.yahoo.com/group/
transgendernews)
Date: August 31, 2002]*

The above article is interesting in that it illustrates two of the positions adopted by so many transsexuals in the light of experience.

Following transition they are normally highly elated: they have achieved what they had wanted for so long and have become women physically as well as mentally.

They are not ashamed and feel strongly that they have a responsibility to speak up for the rights of other women like themselves, women who have had a slightly unusual passage to their womanhood.

They see the issues quite starkly. They are women. They have earned the right to be treated accordingly.

But with the passing of years, they tend to see things a little differently.

Of course, they should have the right to be treated in the same way as other women.

But they also recognise that when other people know of their history, they are not set on a level playing field with other women because they are perceived as women with something different about them.

And, though regrettable, it is an understandable reaction.

TSs at this stage recognise that there are significant advantages in keeping a low profile.

They are delighted that some TSs are highly politicised and dedicated to speaking openly against discrimination against TSs, but see every advantage in remaining hidden within the community and thus avoiding discrimination through the simple expedient of not revealing their history.

Dr Richard's reaction spells out the problem.

Had she not fought for her rights she could perhaps have avoided the notoriety that has attached to her name ever since,

At best she won a sort of Pyrrhic victory and in the process stirred up a hornet's nest and suffered the most painful stings.

So, for any TS in transition or during that post-op period when you are full of excitement at how wonderful it is to be a woman, think very carefully before telling anyone who does not strictly need to know.

Ignore that advice and you will most probably come to regret having done so.

Your story may be fascinating: resist the temptation to sell it to the press. Television and radio chat shows are regularly seeking TSs to appear. Remember that these shows are first and foremost entertainment. The public seems to have an insatiable appetite for seeing 'different' people. These shows seldom consider issues other than at the most superficial level and no matter how useful your envisaged contribution might be, you are unlikely to be given the chance to air it properly.

However, you risk being effectively branded TS and only seen in the context of being a TS.

What do people remember pop singer Dana International for?

Do you remember the name of her Eurovision Contest winning song?

Do you remember what country she came from?

Celebrity can be fun – but it can also

leave a residue of problems, leaving you isolated as a TS and not being recognised as an individual in your own right.

It may be ignoble to let other people stand up and do the fighting for TSs. It may also just be practical common sense.

If you really do believe you are superbly well equipped to campaign openly for TS rights, then by all means do so, but do not complain if the publicity sticks to you and adversely affects your future.

If you do not mind being treated as someone different, as a TS rather than as a woman, then being very open about your past is no problem. Discretion can make your life a great deal easier and help you gain acceptance as a woman rather than as a TS. The choice is yours.

AN INFORMAL GUIDE TO TRANSSEXUALISM FOR EMPLOYERS

A **transsexual (TS)** is a person whose gender dysphoria (feeling of inappropriate gender) is so acute that he/she must take action to match sexual characteristics as closely as possible to his/her perception of gender.

TSs may be pre- or post-operative, male to female (M-F) or female to male (F-M).

Someone accepted as transsexual by a specialist gender psychiatrist, normally following a two-stage referral from a G.P. and a local consultant psychiatrist, is put on a course of hormone treatment and required to live for at least one year in the chosen gender role prior to being considered for corrective gender reassignment surgery (the sex change operation).

The psychiatrist will normally provide a 'to whoever it may concern' letter explaining that the dressing in role is an essential part of the therapy.

This period (sometimes called the 'real life test') enables the TS to have a practical check that his/her chosen course is the right one before committing to irreversible surgery.

The TS inevitably faces a series of stresses: the initial coming to terms with being transsexual; the changeover to living in the new role; confronting the issues with family, friends, colleagues and employers; the effects of hormone therapy; fears of facing ridicule and hostility.

The fact is that transsexualism is a recognised medical condition.

It can be treated successfully and the TS should be accorded the same sort of consideration in the workplace as any other employee.

The fact that the TS in transition is supported by a medical team comprising the gender psychiatrist and the GP does not imply that the TS is in any way deluded or insane.

The truth is that in the case of the transsexual there is a mismatch between body and brain: the brain structure being analogous to that of the opposite sex.

As a general guide it is legally wrong for an employer to dismiss a staff member for being transsexual.

Such conduct has been found by the European Court of Human Rights to be a breach of human rights.

This ruling effectively extends the scope of the Sex Discrimination Act to apply to discrimination against a transsexual on the basis of his/her transsexualism. On the other hand, it may be appropriate to redeploy the transitioning transsexual in the interests of all concerned.

Treatment

The TS is treated by administration of an appropriate hormone therapy regime. In F-Ms this involves male hormone (testosterone) which has the effects of adding muscle mass, stimulating male beard, body hair and male pattern hair growth as well as causing the voice to break. The M-F receives oestrogen which promotes breast development, loss of muscle mass, some fat redistribution and a more feminine facial appearance. Removal of the male beard requires protracted treatment by laser or electrolysis, whilst development of an appropriate voice may need speech therapy, for neither hormones nor gender reassignment surgery will make a male voice sound like a female one. In the early stages of treatment, an anti-androgen may also be prescribed. After an appropriate period of living in role (typically one or two years) the TS is liable to be referred for surgery. The F-M can expect several procedures: bilateral mastectomy (breast removal), oophorectomy, hysterectomy and metoidiplasty or phalloplasty. In other words, they get rid of their breasts, their reproductive tract and can choose the extent to which they wish their genitalia adapted or remodelled. M-Fs have a neovagina modelled from penile and scrotal tissue. Many elect for further procedures to enhance their feminine appearance. Typical procedures include breast implants and facial plastic surgery (nose jobs and face lifts being perhaps the most common).

Prognosis

The TS has typically struggled with transsexualism, feeling wrong in his/her socialised gender role and not necessarily knowing why. If he/she has been a good employee when faced with this troubling problem, there is every reason to expect he/she will be even better once the dysphoria has been resolved, provided that there are no extraneous distress factors such as harassment or discrimination in the workplace.

Practical Implications

As soon as an employee intimates the intention to proceed towards gender reassignment, the employer should discuss the practical implementation of the planned change with the employee and, subject to the employee's agreement, with an agreed Union representative.

Factors to be considered include arranging a staff meeting to explain the situation and the corporate policy regarding it, arranging for amendment of records and setting outline timetables with the TS for ongoing and planned treatments.

Ideally, the TS will give ample advance warning. However, embarrassment may have prevented timely disclosure and a TS may only confront the issue when approaching the time to change over to the new role. Whilst this may be organisationally inconvenient, the good employer should make allowance for such understandable reticence. Indeed, it is important for the employer to understand how fundamental this change really is. It is just as far-reaching as the changes experienced variously through adolescence, pregnancy or menopause. Whilst these are hormonally induced, they are the sort of changes for which we are all groomed by nurture. The TS faces additional hormonally induced changes that affect moods at the same time as having to learn to behave appropriately in the new gender.

Men and women have different behaviour patterns that reflect in body language, vocal inflexion, language, movement, reactions to others, interests and willingness to accept certain tasks.

The changes that turn a girl into a woman, or that trigger the transition from boy through youth to manhood are familiar to us all. They are part of our common evolution through life. It really does not need much imagination to envisage the enormity of the further step from man to woman (or vice versa): a step that radically alters the evolutionary direction the individual has experienced. The TS is preconditioned to take that evolutionary step: it is only in relatively recent times that medical and surgical developments have provided an enabling technology.

Of course, the enormous personal significance of the compulsion to effect this additional evolutionary step should be understood by other staff with whom the TS will come into contact. It is incumbent upon the employer to help promote understanding amongst them in much the same way as it would be to help them understand problems that may affect a wheelchair bound employee, a diabetic, someone who has just experienced a bereavement or a staff member who is facing marital problems.

Unlike the other examples, transsexualism is a somewhat unusual experience. Many people can live through their lives without knowingly encountering a TS and consequently gain their impressions of transsexualism through occasional sensationalist newspaper headlines, chat shows, guests of Gerry Springer and a mish-mash of confused images including drag queens, female impersonators, transvestites and sundry other entertainers.

It is these generally unhelpful images that an understanding employer needs to overturn. Few employers have experience of handling these matters and thus it is often helpful for them to seek advice and, if additionally required, an experienced voluntary counsellor able to make a presentation on the subject to staff and management. TransLiving International is equipped to provide such advice and may be able, by arrangement, to provide or recommend a suitable counsellor. It is worth noting that problems are not resolved by skirting around them, ignoring them or pretending they do not exist. It is far better to deal with them in an open and forthright manner. As a general rule, once people understand the problems faced by a TS in transition, they are usually supportive.

What are the problems?
The TS is likely to be very sensitive and easily upset by incorrect use of the new name or the use of the pronoun inappropriate to the new gender. However, it is not easy for people who have known the TS for a long time to adapt to the change without making an occasional, and perfectly understandable, lapse. Management must be particularly careful to use correct nomenclature and pronouns as soon as the name change has come into effect. Any staff who deliberately persist in using the former name or the inappropriate pronouns should be regarded as wilfully harassing the TS. Although the TS in all probability

aspires to become assimilated into the general community and to be accepted without question in his/her new gender role, it is generally true that during the early stages of living in role the TS can be embarrassingly gauche and seemingly uncomfortable.

It is at this stage that the TS is most vulnerable and in the greatest need of sympathetic understanding.

In the case of the M-F, although presenting as a woman, she may need to permit beard growth for the purpose of enabling treatment by electrolysis. She finds it embarrassing and can be helped if staff understand her predicament.

However, if her work involves dealing direct with the public, the employer should discuss possible options with her (or, if she prefers, with her psychiatrist or counsellor too). Examples of options could include redeployment to tasks not needing public contact when she is growing the beard for treatment, or that she should grow it over the weekend and come in a little later on a Monday after electrolysis.

During the pre-operative 'real life test', the TS will continue under the supervision of the gender psychiatrist (probably involving an appointment every three months) and continue hormone treatment.

The employer should grant sick leave and sick pay for all medical treatments (check ups and surgery) as with any other employee.

M-F TSs may require several hundred hours of treatment by electrolysis. It would be unrealistic to expect this to be treated as paid sick leave, but a model employer should show a helpful attitude towards flexibility of hours, or the granting of agreed levels of unpaid leave to assist the TS in progressing the treatment. She may also need a few hours for speech therapy: this is often prescribed under the NHS and, if so, should be regarded as a legitimate medical treatment.

With reference to use of toilets, it is appropriate for the pre-operative TS undergoing the real life test to use the toilets appropriate to his/her gender presentation.

This should not cause a problem if staff have been made aware of the nature of transsexualism.

We do not recommend fudging the issue by the discriminatory measure of asking the TS to use the disabled toilet facilities, for this merely emphasises the TSs abnormal status in the perception of her colleagues.

It should be made clear that the F-M TS living as a man is to be treated in the same way as any other male employee. Similarly the M-F living as a woman is to be treated as any other female employee.

It is not unusual for some employees to express uncooperative attitudes. Typical examples are:

'As far as I'm concerned he'll always be a bloke in a dress'.

'You can't be a woman unless you bleed.'

'A leopard can't change its spots.'

'He's just a bloke with his rocks lopped off.'

'It ain't a bloke and it ain't a bird either.'

These attitudes usually reflect a management failure to explain the transsexual's predicament and the corporate policy.

You may not be able to guarantee to change the way individual employees think, but you certainly can influence the way they behave.

Corporate Policy
A clear statement of policy sets behavioural guidelines and identifies conduct liable to incur disciplinary measures. As a result, it rapidly becomes embedded in the corporate culture. We would recommend a statement of policy along the following lines:
Transsexualism is a recognised medical condition which is treated by the (Company) in the same way as any other recognised medical condition. Harassment, intimidation or discrimination directed against any transsexual employee is a criminal offence which the (Company) will unhesitatingly report to the police and which may qualify as a serious disciplinary offence meriting summary dismissal. Please note that to reveal that any particular person is transsexual (without their express consent) to anyone who does not know (or need to know) could be deemed discriminatory.
The (Company) recognises the rights of the transsexual employee to change name and gender. The (Company) will afford full recognition of the transsexual's new name and gender immediately upon the transsexual employee effecting the legal name change and change of gender presentation and will amend all payroll and staff records appropriately.
Immediately upon the transsexual employee effecting the legal name change and change of gender presentation, the (Company) requires all staff to treat the transsexual employee in a manner appropriate to the new gender presentation, to use the new name and appropriate pronouns when addressing or referring to the employee.
Immediately upon the transsexual employee effecting the legal name change and change of gender presentation, the transsexual employee has the right to use the toilet facilities appropriate to the new gender presentation.

The role of the Union official
We all know that human nature is imperfect and that no matter how high-minded our ideals, reality often involves having to tackle difficult and unpleasant issues head-on.
The TS may well be over emotional, hyper-sensitive, self-centred and over inclined to bore the pants off everybody by talking about his/her problems. This is a phase that passes, but the Union official may well find himself having to smooth ruffled feathers whilst it lasts.
It helps if he can explain some of the pressures the TS is facing, but he may well need to call on his reserves of tact in the process.

We trust that the above information will be of assistance and will gladly respond to any further enquiries. TransLiving International's Information and HelpLine:
Tel. 01268 583761
(9am to 8pm Monday to Friday)
e-mail: stacy@transliving.co.uk

Employers and Unions are further recommended to read 'Transsexual People in the Workplace: A Code of Practice Regarding Discrimination on Grounds of Transsexualism' published by Press For Change, December 1998. ISBN: 0 9527842 2X, a document produced as part of the UK Parliamentary Forum on Transsexualism chaired by Dr Lynne Jones MP.

OFFICIAL DEALINGS WITH EARLY STAGE TSs AND FTVs

In dealing with early stage M-F TSs (and FTVs), follow the simple courtesy of addressing them as female when they present as female (irrespective of how convincing or otherwise they may be), using the chosen female names and the feminine pronouns concerning them, at the very least when you are in earshot.

Any signing of official documentation will need to be carried out using the male name and title, unless they have been formally changed in a manner accorded legal recognition (i.e. either by Deed Poll or Statutory Declaration). TSs undertaking the real-life test and thus working and living full-time as female would normally have taken the necessary steps to institute such a recognised name change as appropriate.

For these transsexuals, the need to cross-dress is part of their overriding need to become female and identify with female behaviour. This is not just a fantasy for there is evidence that the brain of a male to female transsexual is similar to that of a typical female and quite dissimilar to that of the typical male. Thus the apparently absurd claim to be a woman in a man's body can be viewed as having real justification.

Once living full-time in role, the TS would normally have formally changed her name and her other documentation [passport, driving licence, bank accounts, credit cards, National Insurance card, NHS registration etc.] She should be treated as a woman, although for her own safety should ideally be kept separate from women and men if she needs to be detained. Having changed her name she is entitled to be addressed by her new name and assumed title [Mrs., Ms or Miss].

Please remember, TSs at this time are going through perhaps the most vulnerable phase of their lives. They are experiencing the physical and emotional changes one would normally associate with puberty and menopause all rolled into one short time frame. They have had to come to terms with accepting their need to be female, having generally tried hard to suppress it for years, and most will have found the impact of their change to have been quite drastic.

For many it will have meant loss of employment and employment prospects in the short term; loss of family and friends; for many the loss of home and almost all possessions. Their social standing will have deteriorated significantly (most golf clubs don't like this sort of thing!) and they are faced with the awesome prospect of becoming a person they had never been socialised to become. Many people regard TSs as freaks and/or perverts. Many people have the attitude that whilst it may be amusing to read about them in the papers, you wouldn't want one as a neighbour or having dealings with your children. There is no social or moral obligation for a TS to reveal her condition other than on a strictly 'need to know' basis. There is a relationship of trust however, in which she is entitled to expect that those who need to know will respect her wishes for privacy and do nothing to wilfully endanger it. You may find her behaviour incomprehensible. To her, what she is doing is a necessity. Many would prefer not to be TS:- but it is what they are and they have come to terms with it.

Remember, the pre-op TS on hormone therapy is unlikely to have much sex-drive. The libido suppressing effect of female hormones is frequently potentiated by the taking of an anti-androgen such as Androcur:- an effective chemical castrating agent. Such people are unlikely candidates for the commission of sex offences: yet many people seem to classify them as sexual perverts.

You can usually be reasonably sure you are dealing with a pre-op TS if the name has been legally changed, her documents have been changed and she carries a letter from her Gender Identity Clinic or Psychiatrist. Once she has been on oestrogen based hormones for a few months, you may expect to see obvious evidence of bust development and a softening of facial features atypical of a male of her age.

The post-operative TS has met the criteria for gender reassignment surgery and has had the operation. Her testes have been removed and a neo-vagina formed from residual scrotal and penile tissue. Physically she is a female. She has female genitalia, breasts and general appearance. She perceives herself as female and lives accordingly. She has acquired a female identity and should be treated as a woman at all times. Only her birth certificate reveals her former physical sexual characteristics.

The Government is under pressure to come into line with other advanced European countries and permit a change of the birth certificate too, so that women who have had surgery to remedy physical anomalies (male sex organs) may enjoy the same rights and protections under the law as any other women.

She is not a cross-dresser and the fact that she was once a functional male is irrelevant. She is under no obligation to announce that she is TS and if she does, or if this information is acquired from others, it should be regarded as strictly personal. Any intimate searches should be carried out following the same procedure as required for any other females.

It is always advisable for a TS to be honest with the medical profession, for some treatments appropriate to other women may not be appropriate to her (d & c for example), whilst some investigations not applicable to other women (e.g. checks of the prostate gland) could be relevant.

The post-op TS will normally not be under psychiatric care, for her gender reassignment is viewed as the resolution to her former problems. However, she still needs to continue with hormone therapy [albeit at HRT levels to prevent the onset of osteoporosis] and may need to shave regularly if her electrolysis treatment has not been completed.

If she is in this position, those in authority should be tactful. It is probably better for an understanding female to proffer help with provision of foundation/make up than a male.

Once again, the situation in regard to accommodation needs to be viewed with care. Some post-op TSs can safely share with other women, their gender status not being likely to be called into question. For many this is not the case. They may have problems with beard growth, voice, the need for a wig to cover male pattern baldness, an over prominent Adam's apple or some other giveaway that would almost certainly cause difficulties. Of course, being physically female, they cannot be put with men in any event.

Please remember, despite her history, you are dealing with a female who is liable to be especially sensitive and easily upset. You may instinctively feel she is nothing more than a castrated male, a eunuch feminised by drugs and cosmetic surgery to believe himself to be female. If that is your attitude, please bear in mind that whilst entitled to your opinion, it is not necessarily shared by others and certainly will not be by the TS or the gender specialists who have treated her.

Keep such opinions to yourself and do not behave in such a way as to give her cause to think you are hostile towards her. She is likely to have encountered prejudice and hostility through the course of her transition and it is to be expected that she is liable to be extremely nervous about the treatment she may receive at the hands of strangers.

THE VULNERABILITY OF THE TRANSSEXUAL FEMALE
by Stacy Novak

A lady who normally appears to the world with an air of confidence took a phone call at her home early one morning while just waking to be precise. Her caller was making inquiries of a non-gender movement that she was involved with. After a short while the caller asked the lady's name, on being told it she said, 'you don't sound like a Sally'. Our friend immediately went into an explanation of how she had just come down with a cold, because it was obvious to her the caller had not heard her as a female. When my friend went on to tell me about the conversation with her caller a lady whose hobbies were Tarot, astrology, numerology, etc., it crossed my mind that she could have meant, quite innocently "You don't sound like a Sally but an Anne." The caller immediately, and probably quite inadvertently, made the TS lady think she had been read as a male.

Another girl was cornered by a guy who sidled up to her to say: "I know your little secret." Her immediate reaction was shock horror. What did he know? It turned out he had knowledge of her extremely high profile work (which for security I will not reveal here), save to say that only an extremely intelligent person could do this sort of work. It's such a shame that for many, after totally successful transitions, they can let themselves down by not reacting quickly enough with answers to questions, simply because they have been thrown into a panic.

Upset and panic can bring out the worst in us at any time. A TS lady's past was betrayed by a TS friend who was in an emotional state and saw fit to tell a mutual friend about herself. She also spilt the beans about her friend's status: hence an innocent TS lady felt destroyed.

The mutual friend claims to have no problem with her, accepting her for what she is, yet it is a pity for before the secret came out, she had been accepted as a woman of the gender kind.

She could feel a subtle change in the relationship: an awareness of a different past and thus an awkwardness which prevented normal idle chatter about schooldays, pregnancies, men etc. There is a lesson to be learned. Seldom is it necessary for 'the old person' to be revealed (notably only for medical reasons and a company pension scheme). It seems for some, particularly among the gender scene, a successful transition cannot be kept to oneself. It seems necessary to tell every new kid on the block that *'she* had her op years ago', *she* used to be so and so's partner'.

Of course we need to introduce TS to TS in order that each may compare notes (particularly in the early days), but when a person decides to support the group by paying a once a year visit to a party, for example, is it really necessary to point her out. I'm sure many TVs would be upset if I were to point out: "See that trannie over there, he's the local chief of police/the mayor/ the local councillor etc. It's really a matter of respect for our fellow sisters. Women do not have a monopoly on gossip and much of it is idle chatter that does little harm. However, remember not to reveal certain aspects of other TSs lives:- respect their wish for privacy.

It's hard enough my trying to make people understand about **my** gender. I can tell them my birth certificate says female, I can legally get married, give birth to babies, but now find the need to say I have never been a man and have no wish to be a man, and some still don't understand. Just because I work with the gender community, many people assume I too must be transgendered. It doesn't bother me --- no reason why it should. But I most certainly would feel insecure if I was a TS being questioned like that.

The other courtesy to consider is one of simple respect for the individual: for her right to privacy. I've never understood why, but too many people seem to assume they can ask a TS the most intimate and prying of questions. It seems that many men work on the principle that TSs don't merit being treated in the same way as gender females, and do not deserve to be accorded the same courtesies and degrees of respect as 'whole males'. The simple fact is that they are women whose bodies did not accord with their gender mind-sets. Surgical and medical intervention goes a long way towards remedying the problem. Of course, there are emasculated men who dress up full-time but they are not TSs.

WILL I ALWAYS FEEL INSECURE?

In one word – yes. You may look wonderful, have a fabulous female voice, excellent manner and be the damn near perfect.
But ---
It's always there that but.
There's always someone who can spill the beans about your past. Perhaps a long-standing friend or family member. Perhaps a former colleague. Or the wages clerk. Or the Doctor's receptionist or a bank clerk.
The trouble is that some people need to know.
If you transition in your workplace, then everyone connected with the job will know, and you don't know how many of them will blab and to whom. Does it matter? Is being TS something to be ashamed of?
Yes, it does matter because it affects the way you are treated.
No, being TS is not something to be ashamed of.
The TS must be a little like a spy living under cover in an alien country – seeking to fit in, but always wary of any signs of a problem. No matter how confident she may be, she must always be prepared to cope with the unexpected: to answer whatever question she may be asked in a manner

consistent with her image, and, ideally, in a way that cannot expose her to being discovered to have told a downright lie.

Of course, some TSs take the view that there is no need to hide the truth, no need to lie or be economical with the truth. They spare themselves the feeling of insecurity but perhaps at the cost of being treated as someone different. If you are happy to be known to everyone around as the neighbourhood TS, as 'one of those', the local 'he-she', then being an open book will suit you. But remember, didn't you go through the gender reassignment programme in order to live as the woman you really are – or was it to live as a transsexual who has had the op?

WHERE SHOULD I TRANSITION?

The decision about how to handle the transition process, particularly from the time you change name and gender presentation in order to live full-time in your chosen gender role, is so significant that you should really pre-plan what you are going to do.

If you working within a Company, you will need to consider whether you want to continue with that Company and if so, whether you wish to remain in the same location and doing the same sort of work.

A good employer should offer you support and protection from discrimination and abuse.

Your employer may not be so enlightened.

It is quite possible that the employer's knee jerk reaction to the news of your planned transition may be approaching panic: 'What will other staff think? – What will they do?'

'How will customers react? Will I lose business?'

He may fear that you will look like Dame Edna on a bad hair day and act like Ru Paul.

He may decide he can't take the risks and therefore seek a pretext for easing you out.

He may even go through the motions of being supportive and keep you in your old job. Now that's fine if you are an office worker. But what if your work involves heavy manual labour?

For there is another factor you need to take into account. Whilst your body develops secondary female characteristics, it also loses a great deal of muscle mass and you become significantly weaker physically as well as temperamentally more labile. The result could be that you soon find yourself unable to do the work, yet under great financial pressure to persevere at it.

Even though the employer may be supportive, he cannot guarantee that other staff will be equally accommodating.

They may well be constrained from overtly victimising you, but nevertheless you may quickly become aware that you have become socially ostracised in ways you never expected. For example, it may have been the custom for a clutch of colleagues to go out at lunchtime for a drink and a bite to eat. You had always tagged along whenever you wished.

However, once everyone knows you are going through gender reassignment, you may well find your colleagues disappearing for their liquid lunch and never asking you.

Indeed, it may be apparent, even without anything being said, that they would prefer your room to your company.

Such things might seem quite insignificant now: but when it happens and you are already under a great deal of stress, then such isolation can be extremely hurtful and difficult to cope with.

You may be lucky enough to find some colleagues who are friendly and supportive. Even so, you need to be careful not to dump on them, for your need for understanding and love can become cloying clinginess to someone else.

It is a characteristic of TSs in transition that their focus is very strongly on self. They need a great deal of reassurance that they are doing the right thing, that they look feminine, that everything will work out. They seem to want to justify their actions to anyone who expresses the slightest interest. Perhaps they would do better to remember (as a useful working guide) that the subject most people are most interested in is themselves, not others, and that other people's problems are a real turn-off.

You may think yourself lucky if you are self-employed. After all, you are hardly going to victimise yourself, and there is no reason to think that you could not do just as good a job as before.

You can reassure yourself that customers came to you because of the quality of your work: and that wouldn't change.

Think again.

You have no legal protection as an employee. You have no union fighting your corner. If your customers find what you are doing something of an embarrassment (and it's a racing certainty that they will) then they will desert you in droves.

It's their money to spend how and where they like. They don't have to put up with embarrassment or having to try to be extra careful not to use the wrong pronoun or name.

For most, the process of transition really begins in earnest with the real life test. The hormones are working. The name has been legally changed. The gender presentation has changed. It's a giant step into the unknown, but a step that is being taken to the probable regret of family and friends, for they are losing the person they thought they knew and possibly gaining a complete stranger.

Before taking such a step you really should carefully consider that the step is into something of a minefield. You court the possible loss of family and friends, of your job (or client base) and are liable to experience a significant reduction in your earning potential. Your credit rating will be affected and in losing family you may incur substantial costs (maintenance, alimony etc).

You will be economically more vulnerable, physically weaker and yet be at the threshold of a new (and unfamiliar) life.

You have been socialised as a man. You know how the world works for men.

You will have to learn how it operates for women but without the benefit of having grown up as a girl and having gained the range of experiences such a background would confer.

You are going to face some hefty expenses (even if your op is NHS funded) and may find yourself without work for protracted periods.

And the longer you are without work, the more resentful you will become of the waste of your talents simply because you are TS.

Unless you had shown commendable foresight, it is highly likely that you will need to get rid of your male beard. The only permanent removal method remains electrolysis.

However, the treatment demands that you allow the beard to grow to sufficient length for the operator to be able to see the lie of the hair (angle of growth) in order to probe to the follicle and to be able to get hold of the hair by her tweezers.

It is a long, slow and occasionally painful process.

It needs to be carried out by a skilled operator, for in the hands of somebody slapdash, you could be permanently scarred.

So here's another complication: you'll need to grow your hairs for a couple of days in order to produce a beard that can be worked on.

That can be a trifle difficult for someone living and working as a woman.

At least, if you transition in your old work place, people know you are going through a change and so may be understanding of the fact that on those hair growth days your complexion will leave something to be desired.

Now these problems are not removed by starting your new life afresh in a new area.

You simply avoid some of them.

But you probably won't be able to hide the fact that you are in transition.

A new start is difficult to make.

How do you open a new bank account without revealing things you would prefer to keep to yourself?

How do you get a new job without someone seeking references from the old?

How do you secure accommodation without references?

Of course, you can get casual work or minimum wage occupations where no-one bothers with references. But you may then find yourself somewhat strapped for cash.

You could open a bank account in your new name at your old address and then transfer it to another branch.

Transitioning away may be an option if you have no dependent family.

At least everyone you meet will be relating to you as you are, never having known 'the old person'.

As with so many things about transsexualism, noone can tell you what to do.

All we can do is point out some of the pitfalls and advise you to think very carefully.

The experience of transitioning can be likened to having a nervous breakdown: it takes you over completely.

At the end of it you need to rebuild your life. But that life will be a very different one. Yes, you had a taster during the real life test, but that does not prepare you for ageing as a woman, for possibly putting on a load of weight, for being physically a great deal weaker than before.

To be sure you will have 'been true to yourself' – but count the cost to yourself and others.

If you believe you have no choice, then get on and do it. Be honest with your family and friends: you owe them that. Don't expect them, or anyone else, to understand. It's a bonus if they do.

However, if on weighing up the options you feel that living as a woman is not worth all the hassle, then thank your lucky stars that you realised in time.

So what's the answer about where to transition? Only you can make that decision, but you owe it to yourself and your loved ones to weigh up the pros and cons of the available options

PERSONAL HYGIENE

Stacy writes: One of our young TS ladies (Post Op) came to me recently for help. She had felt sore around her vagina and noticed a rather nasty sour milk smell. I asked whether she had spotted any evidence of a creamy discharge when she took off her knickers for washing --- but apparently not.

She had not had any sexual contacts and felt very embarrassed about the whole thing. I immediately thought her problem was probably thrush and, on telling her my suspicions she reacted with shock at having contracted a venereal disease!

Of course, thrush (candida albicans, a yeast like fungal growth) can readily be sexually transmitted. However, it can also sprout forth as a side effect of the pill (i.e. the taking of female hormones) and of taking antibiotics. Hormones and antibiotics both have the effect of changing the balance of body flora (the nice-sounding word to describe the population of bacteria that thrives on normally healthy people) so that the fungus becomes free to flourish without the usual checks and balances.

The cures:- an application of **live yoghurt** (you can get it from delicatessens or any good supermarket) is a very effective remedy.

Topical application of Canesten (available from any chemist), or Canesten pessaries if appropriate, will quickly clear the problem.

Sexually active ladies should be aware that an infection could be an unwanted souvenir of a pleasurable night and really should check with their local GU Clinic that there have been no other surprises acquired at the same time. They should also remember that clearing their little problem does little good if they immediately get re-infected from their partner passing the infection straight back again. Incidentally, GU Clinics follow strict rules of confidentiality.

THE THINGS THEY SAY ABOUT TS LADIES

Stacy has heard many things over the years --- in this article, she asks you to reflect on some of the frequently encountered comments about transsexuals.

In the years that I have been in and around the TV/TS scene, I've heard many people say many things about others. I have decided to devote this piece to things I have heard TSs remark about other TSs (plus some of the things said about TSs by 'to the gender born' men and women. Although many of the remarks seem cruel, spiteful and downright derogatory, perhaps we could all learn a lot from considering why they were said, what they say about the person talked about and what they tell us about the person voicing an opinion. So, here goes:

She is:
— nothing like a woman.
— like a TV in drag.
— man mad.
— a bitch.
— too big.
— too bald.
— too ugly.
— such a slut.

She doesn't:
— act like a woman.
— have any idea.

You have to:
— drive stupidly
— fake a monthly period.
— lie a lot.
She thinks:
— she is God's gift to men.
— she's superior to real women.
I would never:
— be seen with another TS
— go out with a man shorter than I.
Just look:
— at the amount of make-up she wears.
— her skirts are far too short for her age.
— how she flaunts her silicones.
She only talks:
— about hormones.
— her problems.
— how bad her Op. was.

Things MEN **SAY ABOUT** TSs
— you can't make a woman.
— If I found out a bird I was with had been a bloke, I'd smash its face in.
— I would be interested to see what it's like.
— Good luck to him, I admire his bottle.
— You've got to hand it to him, he's got the balls. At least, he had.
— I wouldn't want to screw him however attractive he looked.
— What guy would want his wedding tackle cut off?

WHAT WOMEN HAVE TO SAY:
— It's an insult to my femininity.
— It makes me sick when they go on about the curse
— Calls herself a Christian?
— I'd kill for those legs.
— Think you're a woman? You don't get that privilege until you bleed!
(taken from a novel, but expressing a familiar theme).

— She looks like a drag queen. A lot of transvestites look more like women.
— She is a real dear.
— I treat her the same as any other of my lady friends.
— Why are their homes so mucky? They keep house like blokes.
— I know one whose house is lovely and tidy.
— My goodness! Her eyebrows make her look like an alien.
— She's nice, but not into feminine things like knitting, sewing, cooking and housework.
She has no idea:
— about make-up.
— how to walk.
— She sits with her legs splayed out wide --- very elegant I don't think.
— She seems to think all men fancy her.
— Why is it that so many of them go through the change and behave like whores?
— She hasn't got a clue how to relate to women as friends. She can't chat.

COMMENT
Isn't it strange how the overwhelming weight of comment is critical. The above represents just a smattering of the things regularly heard. Mind you, there is one comment I keep hearing from TSs when I'm on HelpLine duty — and it really drives me mad. They keep telling me '--- **I think** like a woman".
Bullshit, who are they kidding!
I'm a woman and I don't think like the woman next door, or like any of those down the road come to that. Nor, as a woman, do I think like these TSs.
I think for myself. I think my own way. Of course, there are many beliefs, views and interests I share with others, as too there are likes and dislikes I

have in common with others, male, female, TV, TS, gay or straight, British or foreign, religious or otherwise. I am what I am and am secure in that knowledge.

Too many TSs are so insecure that they are too busy trying to prove that they really are what they purport to be. Why bother? Live it, don't play act. I'm sure we all share the capacity to feel anger, love, despair and hope. No doubt we all can share many of the characteristics generally considered typically feminine. But we are all different.

Even the way we dress and project ourselves reflects this.

How can a TS in tights and sensible cotton knickers say she thinks the same way as I do? I'm comparatively outrageous, an extrovert in nylon and silk scanties — and I prefer stockings too! So ladies, be the woman you want to be and don't make absurd claims of being like all women — for we are all different.

Get things in perspective. You can truly be women, but accept the truth about yourselves at least to yourselves, and admit at the very least to having had a past as a male, no matter how uncomfortable you were in that role. So please, don't come out with that irritating phrase that gets on the wrong side of so many women. You are what you are, and what you are is perfectly valid. Yes, many people can and will accept you as women. But many of those can't and won't tolerate nonsensical claims.

You go through the real life test to show you can adjust successfully. Most women have no need to make such adjustments. You have had experiences that they have never had. Those experiences have helped mould your unique personality as a woman. Yes, you may **have been** transsexual, but you are, or at least aspire to be, female. Be true to yourself, conduct yourself in a manner you can respect: take pleasure in the knowledge you have enjoyed the privilege of being able to reorientate your life in order to be the PERSON you should be. Just two more thoughts for you — (i) if those you meet don't know you are TS, then for God's sake don't go telling them and — (ii) don't behave in a way that makes them question your femininity [e.g. male aggression does not somehow fit the image].

Remember, you have that rare privilege of seeing life from both sides; of experiencing years of being treated as male and then a future as female. Of course the transition can be, and often is, very difficult and you may lose much of what you once held dear. Nevertheless, this major evolutionary change in your life opens an exciting new range of opportunities and challenges at the same time as permitting your personality to develop to its true potential.

In order to help yourself through this process of change, it has been proved time and again that contact with people who understand what you are going through is enormously valuable. TransLiving provides just such sensible, caring support.

We have helped countless TSs through their journey of self realisation, helping with practical advice on health, removal of facial hair, intimate care, symptoms, coping with depression, dealing with employers, family, friends and neighbours, the most cost effective ways to effect a name change, advice on grooming, hair, make-up etc.

BE PREPARED

One of the biggest giveaways to which TSs are prone is lack of preparedness arising from lack of experience of having grown up as girls. A TS ought to be able to converse without awkwardness within a crowd of women when matters such as menstruation, pregnancy, childbirth, sexual intercourse, the size of husbands'/ boyfriends' dicks, fetishism, S&M, cross-dressing, hysterectomies, implants, STD, bringing up children, masturbation, emotions and dirty jokes can crop up at any time.

She must be prepared to field questions about how she feels when she's on, about her pregnancy, her children and her confinement, or about her boyfriend/s and whether she has and what it was like. She needs to understand that women talk far more intimately amongst themselves than do men. Feelings take higher priority than cars, football and politics.

She needs to develop the ability to make small-talk about families, children, parents, the garden, plans to decorate, party planning, fashion, the royal family, the prices in the shops, the relative merits of one supermarket over another and a host of other topics. Ideally, she needs to be able to keep up a steady small-talk dialogue whilst doing other work (a skill exhibited by hairdressers and one which women frequently hone to perfection during the bringing up of their children).

BE PRACTICAL

We often find that TSs forget the simple but not very welcome fact that whilst hormones will give them a bit of a bust, they do not alter the skeleton and do not do much for the hips.
A TS lady is thus liable to be quite narrow on the hips.

Because she is living full time, she expects to be able to go shopping in any shops or stores. But the merchandise in those shops and stores is not likely to be optimised for the narrow-hipped.

TV shops make garments specially to disguise an inconvenient physical shape. You can do well to look in such places from time to time. After all, if the end result is to achieve the effect you seek, does the nature of the shop really matter?

WHAT ARE HORMONES?
Hormone Therapy

Much has been said about hormones and for all the good they do in the treatment of transsexuals, they are dangerous drugs.

Tales of black market suppliers are often heard. Buying from them is extremely dangerous.

Even if your supplier claims to be supplying you quite legally, do not take chances with your life. There is no sense in taking drugs to improve your quality of life if they merely kill you! If taken by the wrong person, without medical supervision, HORMONES CAN KILL.

We must emphasise that hormones are potentially dangerous and can precipitate life threatening complications.

No matter how great the temptation, do not take hormones other than under strict medical supervision.

What are hormones?

They are organic substances secreted by plants and animals. Hormones are chemical messengers which aid the regulation of the body's constant internal environment and this process of regulation is known as homoeostasis.

The female menstrual cycle exemplifies how hormones can regulate the body's internal functions. Hormones known as oestrogens are manufactured in women within the ovaries and then released into the blood stream, from where they are carried throughout the Endocrine System to the body's internal organs. The hormones instruct the organs on the levels of proteins, glucose and water they will need to prepare the body for a possible pregnancy.

The female body periodically produces oestrogens to prepare the organs of the body for possible impregnation. Around the twelfth day of the menstrual cycle the female steroid oestradiol, which is an oestrogen, is at its greatest level. Oestradiol is very like the male steroid testosterone in its chemical structure.

In the past twenty years scientists have made huge strides in the study of genetics, although there are still many unsolved mysteries surrounding the workings of hormones and their effects on the human body, in particular in relation to the sex hormones.

Hormone treatment

Certain hormones have now been synthesised in the laboratory although many scientists are still very wary of making specific claims as to what can and cannot be achieved.

The following hormones are used in the treatment of Transsexuals:-

1.   Oestrogens

The female ovaries, adrenal gland and pregnancy tissues produce these naturally and the male adrenal glands also produce oestrogens but to a much lesser extent than the female. To date there has been no conclusive evidence that the natural oestrogen levels are higher in male to female transsexuals. The levels of oestrogen in females varies during their menstrual cycle but no evidence has been produced to date that the levels in males vary at any time. Oestrogens are used in the treatment of male to female transsexuals to bring about the development of secondary female characteristics.

2.   Progesterones

Again produced by the female, these hormones activate the preparation of the uterus lining to receive a fertilised egg. Progesterones also affect the preparation of the body for the possibility of a pregnancy by the redistribution of body fats, thus giving the body a more female shape. These hormones also affect breast development, the production of milk, assist in the regulation of the female monthly cycle and may also affect psychological attitudes, they decrease sex drive and are assumed to cause pre and post natal depression.

Synthetic versions of this hormone, such as Provera, are now rarely used in the treatment of transsexuals due to these side effects.

3.   Androgens

Males produce these in the form of testosterone, which causes the development of the testes, increased facial and body hair, and development of muscle tissues, and are secreted by the testes and adrenal glands of the male.

The female adrenal glands also produce these but in much smaller quantities, apparently purely for the purpose of regulating the menstrual cycle by combating the female hormones (oestrogens and progesterones).

Testosterone is used in the treatment of female to male transsexuals. Male to female transsexuals are sometimes treated with an anti-androgen hormone (Androcur) which counteracts the androgens.

The following hormones are prescribed for Transsexuals:-
1.   **Premarin**
This is a combination of oestrogens extracted from the urine of pregnant mares.
Premarin usually comes in tablet form, the tablets being coated to prevent absorption into the bloodstream until they are past the stomach, otherwise they may cause an upset stomach. The dosage of this hormone is reduced after surgery. If you have an ethical objection to the methods of producing Premarin, then you should aks your Doctor for a suitalber alternative.

2.   **Ethinyloestradiol and Mestranol**
Again, these hormones are usually given in tablet form and are oestrogens derived synthetically from oestradiol. They may however be injected into the bloodstream, usually at monthly intervals, which ensures the slow release of the hormones to the body. Implants have also been tested but this method of administering these hormones is somewhat unpredictable in its rate of release into the bloodstream. Differences in body weight, metabolism and psychological impact make it almost impossible to accurately predict the precise effect of a given dosage of a specific hormone on an individual body.
Each patient must therefore be thoroughly medically examined by a Specialist before any course of hormone treatment is prescribed.

EFFECTS OF HORMONE TREATMENT
– on breasts, mammary glands and pectoral muscles
Hormone treatment initially causes extra fatty tissue and fluid to be deposited immediately behind the nipple and aureola, which may cause heightened sensitivity around this area. Externally, the area surrounding the nipple and the nipple itself may deepen in colour, and the nipple may appear swollen. There may also be a secretion from the nipple.
The redistribution of fatty tissues in the body may also cause an increase to the hip and thigh measurements, also the back and upper arms. This is partially due to a decrease in the levels of male hormones, causing a loss of muscular development in the body. The features of the face will also soften with the spreading of fatty tissues under the skin, to give a more feminine appearance.

– skin
The skin will often become softer in texture although this is not always so and many transsexuals use good quality cosmetics during the first stages of their treatment.

– hair
The blood supply to the skin is increased by the hormones and this may cause an improvement to the condition of the head hair. Body hair may become softer and more feminine in its appearance. Beard growth will not cease although it will be a little slower. Only electrolysis can permanently remove all traces of male beard.

– voice
Hormone treatment does not alter the voice in male to female transsexuals.

– genitalia
The administration of hormones will cause the testes to reduce in their size, but the penis will not actually waste away, although over a period of time the sex drive will decrease and sterility and impotence will occur.

Psychological Effect
The strains under which most transsexuals live (typically isolation from friends and family, loss of job/income, reduced prospects, marital breakdown etc.) make it very difficult to gauge the direct psychological effects of hormone treatment.

Treatment with hormones is not a 'miracle cure' for gender dysphoria. It is but one part of a programme inevitably involving remedial surgery. Administered in the correct doses, female hormones, oestrogens, will combat the effects of automatic production of male hormones in the male, thus effecting a significant measure of feminisation prior to surgery, although with concurrent administration of an anti-androgen (in effect, chemical castration) the effects of male hormones will be further reduced.

After surgery, the continued administration of oestrogens may well produce some further changes in the appearance and behaviour of the transsexual — perhaps a slight increase in breast size and some further continuation of the changes to fat and body hair distribution.

Many of the more obvious changes are learned rather than a result of hormone treatment, for example, behavioural patterns and voice pitch. The transsexual will need to become at home with all areas of feminine behaviour in order that she may become convincing in her life as a woman.

Nausea
The administration of female hormones in the male may cause nausea, initially, although these symptoms will often disappear as the body becomes used to the treatment. Do seek professional advice if these symptoms occur.

Nails
The body may not be able to absorb vitamins and minerals effectively if digestive upsets are experienced, which may cause nails to crack and split easily.

A course of vitamin supplements may be prescribed by the Specialist to counteract the deficiency, for example Seven Seas Multi Vitamins.

Disease
Hormones will not in themselves cause disease in the transsexual.

Their effect on the endocrine system of the individual may however lower the body's resistance to disease, for example there may be an increased susceptibility to blood disease and related disorders as the hormone treatment affects the bloodstream. Transsexuals really must give their Specialists full details of their medical history, in particular with regard to diseases of the heart, liver or pancreas, cancer, diabetes or disorders of the pituitary gland.

Blood and blood pressure should be tested regularly:- increased levels of oestrogens and progesterones in the body have been known to cause strokes in women.

Side Effects
Bloating and fluid retention, cramps, leg pains, mood change, reduction of sex drive, headaches, nausea, weight gain.

Contra Indications
Sickle-cell anaemia, history of heart disease or thrombosis, liver disorders, some ear, skin and kidney disorders, some cancers. It should be noted that screening procedures (blood tests) should reveal such risk factors for thromboses as Leiden Factor V or Systemic Lupus Erythematosa, which may be present without the TS having known of them.

Caution:
High blood pressure, diabetes, vascular disorders, asthma, depression, kidney disease, MS.

It is advisable for patients taking oestrogens not to smoke and to have regular checks for blood pressure and blood chemistry. Hormone treatment should be stopped before any form of surgery.

Practitioners should check for drug interactions arising from concurrent therapies. Transsexuals should always notify any prescribing Doctor of all the medicines (including over the counter and herbal remedies) that they are taking.

Liver
An increased water retention gives rise to a risk of liver damage.

Atheroma
There may be an increased danger of strokes, gangrene and arteriosclerosis, caused by the administration of anti-androgens, although this risk must be weighed against the desire to lead a woman's life.

As the guidance of a medical specialist is needed for a transsexual to undertake this treatment in Britain, this risk is lessened although it is still there.

Special note: *Androcur, an anti-androgen, has been prescribed to many Transsexuals. It is a high risk drug which can lead to permanent damage to the liver. Its use should be strictly limited in terms of time and dosage. It has fallen out of favour with many Doctors on account of its potential to cause permanent, serious damage. TVs are most strongly urged NOT TO PUT THEIR LIVES AT RISK by experimenting with hormones and anti-androgens. Just remember, hormones can destroy the very sex drive that makes you cross dress and enjoy your TV life.*

TSs should only take anti-androgens in strict accordance with dosage levels specified by their Doctors.

GLOSSARY OF TERMS

Please note that the meanings accorded to the following terms are specific to this work and may be quite different in writings by others.

Cross-dressing: the act of dressing in clothes normally associated with a person of different gender. TVs refer to *being dressed* or *en femme* when cross-dressed.
[Cross-dressing is almost exclusively a male trait. Current psychological theory views it as a behaviour *within the normal range* of male sexuality. It becomes a matter of clinical concern when the cross-dressing becomes a compulsive obsession.]

Passing: a TV or TS is said *to pass* if they pass as a woman in public, without arousing suspicion.

Being read: A TV is said to have been read if someone notices that the 'she' he is presenting as, is really a he.

Transvestism: the practice of cross-dressing.

Transvestite (TV): a person who cross-dresses. TVs include:

Full-time TVs:
– Men who choose to live as women all the time, yet acknowledge that they remain men.
Many of these will adopt female names (possibly changing their names by Statutory Declaration or Deed Poll). They should freely admit their gender status, perceiving themselves as males who prefer to live as females.
Regular TVs
– Men who cross-dress as frequently as they can in their own time.

Occasional TVs
– Men who cross-dress from time to time.

She-males
– Men who have acquired secondary female characteristics through cosmetic surgery and/or hormone treatment. They generally present as women all the time, but retain a full set of working male genitalia. Many she-males are engaged in the sex trade.

Drag Queens
– Men who entertain by parodying women. In the UK, drag queens are primarily a feature of the gay scene.

Transsexual (TS): a person who self identifies as having a persistent wish to live in the gender role other than that suggested by sex from birth and who requires medical and surgical intervention to change the body to make it congruent with the new gender identity.

Gender Reassignment Surgery (GRS): a surgical procedure or set of procedures designed to alter the patient's physical appearance to approximate as closely as practicable to that congruent with the target gender.

Pre-op TS: a transsexual living in chosen gender role but prior to surgical intervention.

Post-op TS: a transsexual who has had gender reassignment surgery (GRS)
No-op TS: a transsexual who declines to have, or is unable to have surgery, but who self identifies as having a mind and body that are incongruent.

The No-op TS is not the same as a Full-time TV, for although they may be physically the same, they have different senses of gender identity.

The real life test: TSs are required to live for a period of at least a year in their chosen gender. This transitional phase is a period of time during which Pre-op TSs live in their chosen gender roles to prove to themselves and their clinicians that the proposed surgical and medical interventions are appropriate.

Transgendered people (TGs): a catch-all term embracing transvestites and transsexuals, she-males and drag queens.

Sex: the attribution of either male or female given to a child at birth on the visible evidence of either penis or vagina (i.e. the evidence that lies between the legs).

Gender: awareness of a person's maleness or femaleness. Gender is perceived by the brain.

Gender identity: the gender with which an individual identifies.

Gender Identity Clinic: a specialist unit to which those with gender identity uncertainties or gender dysphoria may be referred by their local Consultant Psychiatrists following an initial referral from their GPs.

Gender dysphoria: a condition in which there is a lack of congruence between sex and gender.
Gender dysphoric: a person with gender dysphoria.

Gender transient: a person whose self perception of gender keeps changing from one to the other.

Sexuality: a person's preferences regarding sexual relationships.

Heterosexual: a person whose sexual relationships are only with members of the opposite sex.

Homosexual: a person whose sexual relationships are only with those of the same sex.

Bisexual: a person whose sexual relationships can be with either sex.

We have generally observed the following style conventions:
−   Transvestites are referred to by the gender specific personal pronoun of their sex at birth.
−   Transsexuals are referred to by the gender specific pronoun relevant to their gender role in daily life.
−   Use of the non-gender specific plural form (their and theirs) when referring to a person of either gender in the singular in preference (generally) to such constructions as his/her or hir.

CONTENTS

2   STACY NOVAK WRITES ABOUT TRANSLIVING INTERNATIONAL – AND INSIGHTS

•

SECTION ONE
TRANSVESTISM

A series of articles concerning transvestism and its impact on the transvestite and those around him.

•

4   **TRANSVESTISM**
4   *What is transvestism?*
4   *Can it be cured or treated?*
4   *Broken promises, deceit and guilt*

5   **A CROSS-DRESSING PARTNER – THE SUDDEN DISCOVERY**
6   *He likes cross-dressing so he must be gay!*
6   *He is a man who likes pretending to be a woman, so he must be bi-sexual?*
7   *He's not nuts! (or if he is, it's not because he's a TV)*
7   *It's not immoral*
7   *It's not illegal*
8   *It is a part of his character, not behaviour of his choosing*

9   **WHAT IS A TV?**
9   *Sexuality is a separate issue*
10   *A TV is for ever – probably*

10   **COPING WITH A TV PARTNER**
10   *Agreeing terms and conditions*
11   *Sex and the TV*
12   *Why did he get married and have a family?*
12   *He doesn't want to be a woman*

12   **WHY DO TVS DRESS LIKE TARTS?**

13   **A TRANSVESTITE IN THE FAMILY:**
13   *Problems for the female partner*
15   *Problems for a male partner*
15   *The effects of a parent's transvestism on his children*

16   **THE CROSS-DRESSING CHILD**
17   *Where did I/we go wrong? Why has he turned out like this?*
17   *What can be done about it? Can he be cured?*
18   *Does it mean he is gay? Is it an illness? Is it a mental sickness? Is he a pervert? Will he grow out of it?*
19   *Mixing with others --- the TV scene*
20   *How do I know he is not a transsexual?*

20   **TV FANTASIES AND THEIR POSSIBLE EFFECTS AND COMPLICATIONS**
21   *The TV in the workplace*
23   *TVs and Doctors*
23   *--- and Ministers of Religion, Therapists and Counsellors*

24   **THE LONELINESS OF THE SINGLE TV**
26   *Hormones – a cautionary note*

•

SECTION TWO

An overview of transvestism, transsexualism, various types of crossdressing and anomalous

	gender behaviours
	•
28	**AN OVERVIEW OF THE TRANSGENDERED AND HOW THEY PRESENT.**
29	*Full-time TVs*
30	*She-males*
30	*Transgenderists (aka gender transients)*
30	*Transgendered*
30	*A transsexual (TS)*
31	*Early stage M-F TSs (pre-op TSs)*
31	*The post-operative TS*
32	*Summary*
32	**DISCRIMINATION ON THE GROUNDS OF GENDER DIFFERENCE**
40	*A sex difference in the human brain and its relation to transsexuality*
40	*Recommended reading*
40	**UNDERSTANDING INTERSEX STATES**
41	*Androgen Insensitivity Syndrome*
42	*Five-Alpha Reductase Deficiency*
43	*The Hermaphrodite*
44	*Klinefelters Syndrome*
45	*XYY Mosaic*
46	*Congenital Adrenal Hyperplasia*
46	*Testicular Feminisation*
46	*Turners Syndrome*
47	*Cloecal Extrophy*
47	*Individuals and their Parents*
49	*References*
49	*Further information*

SECTION THREE

This section is devoted to advisory articles of relevance to both transsexuals and transvestites. Many of the issues raised are more pertinent to transsexuals and full-time transvestites.

•

52	**COMING TO TERMS WITH YOURSELF**
53	**FITTING ROOM PROTOCOL**
53	*Communal fitting rooms*
53	*Use of ladies loos and fitting rooms*
53	*Duty of care*
55	**THE FEMALE VOICE**
57	**PRESENTING YOURSELF**
58	**HIDING THAT BOTHERSOME BEARD**
59	**STACY'S RECOMMENDED SELECTION OF BASIC BEAUTY PRODUCTS**
60	*I'm a woman now --- I don't need all this make-up –*

•

SECTION FOUR

This section looks at transsexualism, how it impacts on others, how they can try to understand it and some of the problems specific to transsexuals

•

62	**A TRANSSEXUAL SON: AN INFORMAL GUIDE FOR PARENTS**
63	**THE YOUNG TS**
70	*What help is there for parents, families and friends of TSs?*
70	*Is there anything that will stop this Transsexualism?*
71	*How about my other children and the reactions of other people?*
71	*What should I do now?*

72	A TRANSSEXUAL PARENT		REGRETS FIGHTING FOR RIGHT TO PLAY (CANADA)
73	AN INFORMAL GUIDE TO THE OP.	89	AN INFORMAL GUIDE TO TRANSSEXUALISM FOR EMPLOYERS
78	WHERE TO GO FOR THE OP.	90	*Treatment*
		90	*Prognosis*
78	PRIVATE OR NHS --- WHICH IS BETTER?	90	*Practical Implications*
		91	*What are the problems?*
79	FREQUENTLY ASKED QUESTIONS. Dr Russell Reid provides the answers	93	*Corporate Policy*
		93	*The role of the Union official*
		94	OFFICIAL DEALINGS WITH EARLY STAGE TSs AND FTVs
79	*Oestrogel*		
79	*Finasteride or Proscar*		
80	*Frequency of blood chemistry tests pre-operatively*	96	THE VULNERABILITY OF THE TRANSSEXUAL FEMALE
80	*Frequency of blood chemistry tests pre-operatively*	97	WILL I ALWAYS FEEL INSECURE?
81	*Long term after care*	98	WHERE SHOULD I TRANSITION?
81	*Post-operative hormone preparations and doses*		
		101	PERSONAL HYGIENE
81	WHEN IS IT BEST TO HAVE THE OP?	101	THE THINGS THEY SAY ABOUT TS LADIES
82	WHAT ABOUT OTHER FEMINISING SURGERY?	104	BE PREPARED
83	I THINK I AM A TS – BUT HOW DO I KNOW?	104	WHAT ARE HORMONES?
		104	Hormone Therapy (cautionary note)
83	GOING DOWN THE TS ROAD – WHY IT'S OFTEN AN ALLURING PATH TO DISASTER	105	1. *Oestrogens*
		105	2. *Progesterones*
		105	3. *Androgens*
		106	*Hormones prescribed for Transsexuals*
86	TRANSSEXUAL ATHLETE ADVISES CYCLIST TO QUIT – FORMER TENNIS STAR	106	EFFECTS OF HORMONE TREATMENT
		106	*– on breasts, mammary glands*

	and pectoral muscles
106	*– skin*
106	*– hair*
107	*– voice*
107	*– genitalia*
107	**Psychological Effect**
107	**Nausea**
107	**Nails**
107	**Disease**
108	**Side Effects**
108	**Contra Indications**
108	**Caution**
108	**Liver**
108	**Atheroma**
108	**Special note:** *Androcur*
109	**GLOSSARY OF TERMS**
111	**INDEX**
115	*Membership application/ donation form for photocopying.*

TransLiving International, PO Box 3, Basildon, Essex, SS13 3WA, United Kingdom

TransLiving International
MEMBERSHIP APPLICATION

Please accept my first year's subscription as:

☐ FULL MEMBER (UK)   £30.00 (*OR 5 MONTHLY PAYMENTS OF £6.00)
☐ OVERSEAS MEMBER (EC)   £32.50
☐ OVERSEAS MEMBER (OTHER)   £35.00

Please pay by credit card, cheque drawn on a british bank, british postal order or girocheque. For payment by bankers draft, please e-mail, fax or phone for instructions.
*The easy payment scheme is designed to help in cases of genuine hardship. Please send proof of receipt of State benefit.

I enclose my payment for membership of ☐

I enclose a support donation of ☐

Please charge my credit card in the sum of ☐ for membership

Please charge my credit card in the sum of ☐ as a donation

Please charge my ☐ Visa   ☐ Access/Mastercard   ☐ Connect

Card Number ☐☐☐☐ ☐☐☐☐ ☐☐☐☐ ☐☐☐☐

Expiry date _____ Signature _____ Date _____

Femme name [   ]   Date of birth: [   ]

The following should show exactly how you wish us to address items posted to you:

Name   [   ]
Address [   ]
         [   ]
         Post Code: [   ]   e-mail: [   ]

Telephone Number including dialling code [   ]

Wife/Partner's name (please include on membership) [   ]
(withhold if likely to cause embarrassment)

Office use only:

---

please sent to:- TransLiving P.O. Box 3 Basildon, Essex, SS13 3WA
It would greatly help reduce Group overheads if UK members could include four first class stamps to assist with postage of your introductory pack.

TransLiving International contacts:

Write to: Stacy Novak at:
TLI,
PO Box 3,
Basildon,
Essex SS13 3WA,
UK

Information and HelpLine:
Tel. 01268 583761
(9am to 8pm Monday to Friday)

e-mail: stacy@transliving.co.uk

Website: http://www.transliving.co.uk

TransLiving International services:
Counselling
Befriending and mutual support
Publishing: via both web and print
Promoting information exchange and social contact
Education and information provision
Liaison with professional agencies
Representation of the interests of the transgendered
HelpLine support

TransLiving International is funded by voluntary contribution, membership fees and such other charitable donations and sponsorship monies as are, from time to time available.